W9-AEW-786

RELIGIOUS PATHOLOGY AND CHRISTIAN FAITH

BR110
L62

RELIGIOUS PATHOLOGY AND CHRISTIAN FAITH

by

James E. Loder

THE WESTMINSTER PRESS
Philadelphia

AUG 22 1986

108822

COPYRIGHT © MCMLXVI W. L. JENKINS

All rights reserved — no part of this book may be reproduced in any form without permission in writing from the publisher, except by a reviewer who wishes to quote brief passages in connection with a review in magazine or newspaper.

LIBRARY OF CONGRESS CATALOG CARD No. 66-11918

Published by The Westminster Press®
Philadelphia, Pennsylvania

PRINTED IN THE UNITED STATES OF AMERICA

To Arlene

Contents

Section Three

CONFLICT AND CREATIVITY

Section Four

CONCLUSIONS

Preface

The major ideas presented here were first the concluding substance of a doctoral dissertation. The principal reason for putting this interdisciplinary statement in publishable form is that in current years diverse "alien" disciplines have found their way into theological curricula without their being critically evaluated in terms of their relatedness to the classical theological disciplines. The present, relatively peaceful coexistence is institutionally and "politically" valuable, but the problems involved are a constant goad to thought and evidence of unfinished business. The broader need is for interdisciplinary studies that can speak responsibly to several areas such as social ethics, public education, and psychiatric theory and practice, where theological and behavioral thought are inevitably and often inextricably involved. Therefore, the aim of the study is to develop an epistemology that is both theologically and behaviorally sound, but that at the same time has enough integrity of its own to give it critical and constructive power both for its parent disciplines and for other interdisciplinary studies. The book is programmatic in the sense that this epistemology has yet to be related to sociocultural theory and to concrete institutional contexts through supplementary studies.

The book is developed in the following manner. Chapters I, IV, VII, IX, X, and XI state the major conclusions of the argument; the intervening chapters present the roots of the argument through the critical and comparative analyses of the works of Kierkegaard and Freud. The negative and positive dimensions of the epistemology are most succinctly stated in Chapters IV and IX, respectively.

For their advice and critical appraisals, I am grateful to the members of my dissertation committee, Profs. Hans Hofmann, David C. McClelland, and Richard R. Niebuhr. I wish to thank the Danforth Foundation and the staff of the Menninger Foundation for making possible a year of concentrated study and research in the areas that relate to this book. I have appreciated the responsiveness of my students and the encouragement of my colleagues, in particular D. Campbell Wyckoff, to whom I have addressed many of the ideas presented here. I would also like to express my gratitude to Princeton Theological Seminary for its aid, in countless ways, in preparing the manuscript. To my wife who has patiently read and reread these pages with a critical acumen and supportive manner which have been invaluable, I am especially grateful.

J. E. L.

Princeton, New Jersey

CHAPTER I

Introduction:

OBJECTIONS TO WRITING THIS BOOK

Scholars in psychology and related fields are no longer repulsed by what Sigmund Freud uncovered. Freud's impact upon his world was revolutionary, but we are now in the post-Freudian era. Beyond Freudiana, we have Freudian clichés and facile observations running through the fabric of everyday speech. The Oedipus complex, infantile sexuality, the father image, and the entire Freudian armory constitute the language system shaping the many American multimillion-dollar projects in mental health. It might even be observed that, instead of discovering the nature of mental illness, many of these Freudian notions have become instructive to those who need to know " how to get sick." Thus, on the levels of popular speech and practice and on the several levels of clinical research, those words and concepts which scandalized Victorian social and professional circles have achieved cultural autonomy and have become a decisive influence among the forces that are molding the cultural, social, and personal life of Western civilization.

Professors and practitioners in the several anthropological disciplines are presently engaged in a reexamination of the relationships between the disciplines fathered by Freud and the more time-honored patterns of thought and behavior. Psychology, sociology, anthropology, education, philosophy, and history have all inherited both insight and agitation from Freud's thought. Even the Christian church, one of the principal targets of earlier psychoanalytic derision, has undertaken a critical assimilation of these insights and theories which were intended to undermine its existence. The general concern of this volume is this last particularly unique and complex assimilation, which is no longer a matter of preference but a matter of cultural fact. Factual as it is, outside of some specialized work in pastoral care, very little has been accomplished in laying down guidelines for the evaluation of this assimilation and for the responsible and creative use of it.

The first problem in the assimilation of Freud is finding precisely how, in the vast range of Christian thought, his work can contribute its massive insight without committing an equally massive reductionism of that thought. The second problem is relating Christian thought to Freud in such a way as to avoid merely consigning his views to a Biblical category, to a subdivision of a minor doctrine, or to the category of updated heresy. That is, Biblical and theological reductionisms are to be eschewed equally with psychological reductionisms. Methods of correlation between Freud and Christian thought which say that Freud goes just so far and then the Christian religion takes over must be eliminated immediately as simply not facing the issues.

Of course, an assimilation of Freud that permits his insights to enter the very heart of Christian thought can be threatening even when assurances against reductionism are set forth at the beginning. Therefore, there will immediately be objections that should be met at the outset in order to delineate the author's perspective as clearly as possible.

The most obvious objection to such a project is also the most significant. The insights of psychoanalysis are conceived and elaborated under clinical conditions with respect to persons whose "positive mental health" has failed. Consequently, the facts and theories of psychoanalytic thinking are pertinent only to the conditions under which they arose. Thus, Christian thinking cannot utilize psychoanalytic models without at least implicitly presupposing that Christians have in some measure lost their positive mental health. Logically this objection would declare that an application of psychoanalytic insights to persons whose positive mental health is intact violates not only the presuppositions of the thought system itself but also the subjects to whom it is to be applied.

Behind this line of thinking are two myths that need to be exposed. The first is the myth of normalcy. This myth divides mankind into two classes: the sick and the healthy; and then it attributes higher moral stature to health than to sickness. The word that fuses the natural condition of health with the possession of moral stature is "normal." This word is not the equivalent of "average" since it lacks the pejorative power of the latter. It is, rather, the name of whatever is being done at the time by most of the people who might possibly be doing it. "Normalcy" designates an uncritical conceptual confusion of four clearly distinguishable realms of human behavior: biological and psychological functioning, moral judgment, and social interaction. It is a myth in that it purports to be true, to say something significant, in all four realms at once, while at the same time retaining an immutable, essential truth that is mysteriously independent of any of the realms to which it purports to speak. Unfortunately, the myth of normalcy does not qualify either as a uniquely interdisciplinary notion or as an instructive myth in the best sense of that term. Its error is the confusion of transcendental truth with custom.

The real dangers inherent in the notion of normalcy are not primarily due to its uncritical, unreflective confusion of certain realms of behavior but rather to its variability at a high level of abstraction. By this I mean the biological, psychological, moral, or social content of the notion changes from one era of history, one social order, or one subgroup to another, and, wherever it is employed, the myth remains an object of devotion. It is commonplace to say that what is true or appropriate or meaningful in one society may not be so in another. Cultural anthropologists have proved this point in many subtle ways; language and value differences make it obvious. So it should be obvious that the content of " normalcy " varies from one set of circumstances to another. Evidently it is expressive of, but not informing for, the individuals and society from whom its content is derived.

What is " normal," then, has no essentially moral qualities; it is epiphenomenal, not criterional. Furthermore, its critical comments on the biopsychological sphere are made from a standpoint of social interaction, and its critique of social practices is based simply on other more widely held social practices. It seems to lack any essential truth that would qualify it as a useful myth. "Normalcy," then, is a phenomenon that is subject to sociocultural investigation, but it is not a standard for judgment or a basis for action. The conclusion is this: since any given content for normalcy has the approximate canonical status of a unison yawn, it can hardly mark the line where psychoanalytic thought should leave off and theological thought begin. Indeed, as the subsequent discussion will maintain, there is no such line that can or should be drawn.

If the first myth fails for lack of appropriate differentiations and for the creation of a mercurial abstraction, the second myth commits the contrasting errors of rigidified differentiation and glorified reductionism. This myth would support the statement that theology and psychoanalysis are separate disciplines with different objects of study, different methods, different criteria for judgment, and different practical concerns. The myth of disciplinary purity that eviscerates the academic world would, therefore, not permit anything but the cleanest line between Christian theology and correlative theories and practices of psychoanalysis. Perpetuation of this myth is dependent upon two classical errors in thought: (*a*) the genetic fallacy, and (*b*) what Alfred North Whitehead called the "fallacy of misplaced concreteness."

a. The Aristotelian boundaries between the disciplines to which we still largely adhere were based upon seemingly self-evident distinctions. Such distinctions pertained to the kinds of objects available for investigation, between organic and inorganic matter, mind and body, the group and the individual; and between all these categories and metaphysics, the differences were as much "givens" as were the content of each discipline. In contemporary thought and research, however, none of these differences is taken for granted, and in every case it can be shown that the self-evident distinction is not only superficial but misleading. Research in biochemistry has been able to reproduce from inorganic matter the structure and functioning of the gene, the basic unit of organic human life; psychological research, especially with epileptics, has made it possible to reproduce by electrical stimulus not only motor responses but idiosyncratic patterns of thought; the major insights being made into the psychological functioning of the individual are based upon the biosocial models of man in which he is interpreted as a "node" on a sea of interacting, interdependent forces. As mentioned above, all the sciences – physical, biological, and behavioral – have so radically reduced the area of metaphysics that for some years the prevailing philosophical thought of Britain and the United States has declared that metaphysical statements are literally nonsense, and only "analytical" propositions, and those directly subject to sense verification, are meaningful.

In view of these contemporary developments no one should hold that the disciplinary purity could be retained on the basis of the object to be investigated. If he does so, he commits the genetic fallacy by validating contemporary distinctions merely on the basis of their original utility and their acceptance in past ages.

b. There are, of course, other distinctions between the disciplines that would seem to preserve their purity in spite of the breakdown of the evident distinctions between kinds of objects to be investigated: the nature of the questions addressed to the object studied, the method of getting and verifying answers to those questions, and finally, the "context of explanation." The last category consists of the basic assumptions of the investigator that are derivative from the age in which he lives, the particular cultural area in which he is working, and, not least, the opinions of his colleagues, "authorities in the field"; this category provides the investigator with learned but merely operational limits for his curiosity. Beyond these limits a statement or proposition is not meaningful; short of these limits the investigator's curiosity is probing and restless. The context of explanation precedes – in the life of the investigator – not only the questions asked but even the predisposition to undertake any particular investigation. Since this is the case, the disciplines are consensually validated, systematized points of view, but they are essentially "points of view" which may be shifted from one "object" to another almost at will. Thus, one may examine the psychology of metaphysics just as he may investigate the metaphysical implications of the structure of inorganic matter. Indeed, all that exists may come under scrutiny from many imagined viewpoints, including some that have not yet been conceived. The radical distinctions between disciplines come into serious question when not only the objective basis for the distinctions has vanished, but also the vestiges are fundamentally points of view repeatedly queued up by "appropriate" questions, standardized methods, and predetermining contexts of explanation. To maintain a priori that disciplinary purity exists is to reify the distinctions between objects, the questions asked, the methods employed, and/or the explanatory contexts. This is the fallacy of thought that Whitehead called "misplaced concreteness."

Disciplinary distinctions are facts of our cultural life; they, like normalcy, are phenomena to be recognized and studied, but they have no more than an operational status, except for persons who implicitly commit this fallacy. There is no essential core of truth in the "fact" of disciplinary distinctions, so there is no real myth here in the sense that a myth enshrines an immutable verity in a fanciful exterior. Disciplinary distinctions are fanciful but not revelatory; imaginary but not imaginative. Like a myth of normalcy, the myth of disciplinary purity is an empty myth. The disciplinary subdivisions of the academic world adhere to each other like the levels of Peer Gynt's onion; one may peel it hopefully, one disciplinary layer after another, but the eventual cause for weeping is the discovery that the "onion" lacks a central core.

This should suffice to expose the myths behind the first objections to this book. It remains to be pointed out that these myths — even though they are empty — do serve an organizational purpose. In whatever society they exist — a national social order or the society of one academic community — they establish the horizon of human accomplishment and the systematic procedures by which a bit of knowledge may be verified or a practice certified. As such, these two myths are both complementary and counteracting. Normalcy sets the limits within which the diversity of separate interests and procedures may function; the diverse disciplines, on the other hand, offset the boring regimentation of "the consensus of opinion." However, when disciplinary distinctions are reified, these distinctions become part and parcel of normalcy and can only offset normalcy in a "normal" way.

This is not to say that in academic communities and elsewhere the disciplinary boundaries are not also maintained by vested interests of various sorts, but the distinctions as they presently exist and their radical reaffirmation are plausible only because the distinctions are part of the "normal" state of affairs.

The foregoing analysis should make it evident that the first objection to this book is proffered out of a set of concerns that center around social utilitarianisms and a viewpoint that has covertly – and perhaps unwittingly – devitalized diversity. To hold fast to a set of distinctions between the disciplines because it is normal, and to defend normalcy by presupposing hard-and-fast distinctions between the disciplines is in itself circular. Such reasoning invites even greater criticism when both normalcy and disciplinary distinctions are recognized as empty myths; one balloon cannot very well ballast another if each is filled with gas lighter than air.

Patterns of normalcy change, and disciplinary boundaries shift as increasingly more penetrating insights are made into the nature of the existing phenomena. This is the first presupposition of this volume and the one that will permit me to lay aside popular considerations of normalcy and rigid disciplinary distinctions for the extent of the phenomenological investigation that comprises the central portion of the argument.

A second presupposition grows out of a second objection. It may be feasible to allow the insights of psychoanalytic thought to penetrate the substance of Christian thinking, but psychotherapy is a form of education, or " reeducation " as Freud called it. Surely – so goes this objection – the Christian faith is not something that can be learned, nor can it be induced through the process of redirecting the drives of a natural man as takes place in psychoanalytic practice. Faith is received by grace, and grace not only is not man's to administer but it conforms man to that faith which is not of himself; it shapes him into the basic form of humanity, which is the man Jesus. The only valid education, then, is an enrichment of the faith that has already been delivered; and surely psychotherapy can do little more for a Christian than to help him appreciate and rely upon the new life which is in him, but which for some reason or other he is unable to live out. Therefore, the objection concludes, it would be better to leave theological integrity intact by not cluttering it with insights from the " man sciences." Worse than that, such an interdisciplinary venture might commit the Pelagian or semi-Pelagian error of suggesting that man can, in and by himself, overcome his sin as well as his sins.

While this objection bears some similarity to the first in its concern for disciplinary integrity, it has seemingly quite a different view of normalcy. The criterion of normalcy here stands both apart from and over against the epiphenomenal normalcy of social organization; there would seem to be no naturalistic fallacy in this assertion. The criterion is absolute, revealed, and so independent of the natural as to be impossible for any human life finally to attain unto it. But if the human essence in Jesus is so pristine and undefiled, does not its human relevance (without which it is what we derisively call " utopian ") lie in its ability to conform man anew, to change not only certain behavior patterns but also the very structure of his personality? If it were not for this power to change human life, surely the Christian faith and all its theological bastions would be little more than a shared fantasy which is compulsively rationalized century after century. It would not even be a "healthy" utopianism, since it would not fall on the near side of the horizon of "normalcy." As an illustration of the importance of structural change, note that it was precisely because of Freud's success in changing the structure of psychic functioning through psychoanalytic techniques that he could denounce other methods which claimed the same ability and, in particular, deride the Christian church for pepetuating a "mass neurosis."

If the concrete claim that Christianity makes for human society is the ability to change human life, it is not the integrity of theology that needs further elaboration, but rather it is the integrity of human change that needs closer scrutiny and more penetrating insight. It cannot merely be said that the kind of change which is uniquely Christian is that which enables one to assert and maintain the tenets of Christian theology. This would be to say that the integrity of Christian change lies in the verbal assertions that were made after the change took place, which is to place the entire burden for defining the integrity of the change upon the integrity of theology. But theology cannot bear this burden because the integrity of theology itself is *sui generis*, and as such it has no autonomy different from any other elaborate rationalization of a belief or shared opinion that is held and defended a priori. It must, rather, be maintained that theological assertions are expressive of psychological events just as definitely — though in a different way — as they are descriptive of the nature of the Godhead and supernatural events. One is able to make theological affirmations because of changes that have been wrought in the structure of his personality. Affirmations of any sort — theological included — are expressions primarily of the personality; only secondarily do they express the supernatural truth which in theological circles sets everyone's curiosity at rest. It is to the analysis of the psychological substratum for theological assertions that a major portion of this book is directed. The assumption that such a substratum may be found and defined is, of course, a presupposition of the entire discussion.

Thus, in final answer to the second objection, it is necessary to point out that to analyze the psychology of change does not necessarily presuppose that such a change could be reproduced (the ultimate objection to Pelagianism). It may, however, reveal the nature of psychic change — or part of it — which is associated with becoming Christian and the ways in which obstructions to such change may be removed. It may also uncover human capacities that are being abused or even emasculated by our ignoring the tight interdependence of verbal forms and psychic structure (Biblical fundamentalism is psychologically far deeper than the words in which its defense seems to be locked). When Christianity becomes a lived fact, it becomes a matter of psychic change and interpersonal engagement involving both language and thought. As long as there is no necessary causal connection between what is done on a human level to reveal man to himself (at any stage in his development) and the action of Divine Grace, Pelagianism is not a problem.

It has been assumed in the past that the absence of such a necessary connection eliminated the value of understanding the nature of Christian change and the importance of efforts that might be exerted to alter the course of human development and to introduce the conditions for the creative realization of the human potential in each individual. Of course, no educational, counseling, or homiletical program could ever presume to do what Divine Grace does; but, having said that, I must emphasize the positive correlate: precisely because the grace of God manages to maintain its autonomy, initiative, and formative power quite apart from human activity, it impinges upon us fully to become responsible men in the world. By so becoming, we in no way detract from the integrity of God's nature; on the contrary, we are better enabled to avoid distortions of our humanity and to lend maximum personal reinforcement to the grace of God once it has been delivered to us.

The objector could rush at this last assertion, reminding us that the definition of "man" is Jesus, in whom we find essential man, and so, he could say, we have merely talked in a circle around the point at which we should have begun, namely, Christology. But this draws us back unnecessarily into theology as a discipline from which we have sought to extricate ourselves for the purpose of relating psychic functioning to theological affirmations. Therefore, the definition of the term "man" – when it is *also* understood at the level of psychic functioning – is an open question. Moreover, it is the question, the concrete answer to which grounds theology in human life as it is now being lived, not solely in human life as it has been revealed in the humanity of Jesus Christ.

Yet the distinction between life as it is lived and life as it has been revealed is only partially valid. The revelation is not mere history and documents, but an expression of life as it is lived. Since all human expressions are formative of the expresser, as well as expressive of his needs, drives, instincts, beliefs, and intentions, theological language and other types of "revelatory" behavior are in their unique way always at work shaping the agent of such language and action. If, then, one is to some extent formed by how he expresses himself, it must be granted to the objector that man-in-general is not sufficient focus for this inquiry. Theological assertions about man's nature must be allowed to direct this study; indeed, in its perseity — apart from such focus and direction — a psychic description of man's nature says little or nothing about the theological doctrine of man. Therefore, the issue at hand may be stated as follows: How is the ultimate form of man, Jesus, related to the proximate form of man, the human psyche? In the words of Søren Kierkegaard, " What I am concerned about is the 'how,' the personal reinforcement of the proclamation. Without that, Christianity is not Christianity."

At this point the discussion runs headlong into a third objection, which cannot be fully dealt with in the compass of this book. This objection concerns the matter of methodology, and it may be stated as follows: Will not the very investigation of " how " in itself predispose the discussion to reach certain conclusions that are products of the approach rather than conclusions reached from an investigation of the relevant phenomena? The methodology of this discussion will have to be presupposed, since I have expounded it at some length elsewhere.[1] The method — as distinct from the methodology — of the discussion is calculated to avoid as many unexplained generalities in as short a compass as possible; it must therefore utilize known contexts and assume that he who is in doubt at some point may refer to the primary sources.

Freud's concern with the human determinants of religious experience has been made famous and notorious by a series of writings that includes *Obsessive Acts and Religious Practices*, *Leonardo da Vinci: A Study in Psychosexuality*, *Totem and Taboo*, *The Future of an Illusion*, and *Moses and Monotheism*. These and portions of other relevant writings, including his cases, permit his thought to be focused upon phenomena that are of decisive importance for Christian thought.

The man whose work is of central historical and contemporary systematic significance for Christian thinking, and whose work also comes to focus upon the same phenomena, is Søren Kierkegaard. He stands close to the center of neoorthodoxy in his influence upon Reinhold Niebuhr and Karl Barth. His influence upon contemporary philosophy is widespread in various brands of "existentialism," but in his impact upon Heidegger and Bultmann he has come to have a vital influence upon Biblical theology and hermeneutics. Moreover, his influence has extended into psychiatric theory through the writings of Ludwig Binswanger and Rollo May. Quite apart from a detailed evaluation of his influence upon theology, Biblical studies, philosophy, and psychology, his analyses have had pervasive and positive formative significance which seems to have cut across several disciplinary boundaries.

By colligation, correlation, and functional analogy these two representative positions will be studied and critically utilized in order to penetrate more deeply into the nature of human change in Christian experience. The locus of human change in this interdisciplinary inquiry is in the patterning of the phenomena of consciousness.[2] The guides for evaluating the Christian assimilation of Freudian thought and for the responsible and creative use of that assimilation emerge directly from the analysis and description of predominant patterns in consciousness. Consequently, the plan of the argument will be initially to arrive at an analysis of consciousness, first in its distortions and then in its reality, and finally to develop its implications.

SECTION ONE

Religion Against the Individual

SINCE ONE AIM OF THIS VOLUME IS TO BRING THE VIEWpoints of Kierkegaard and Freud into a mutually enlightening relationship, it must be demonstrated that their respective positions have not been falsified for the sake of the correlation. Also, such a demonstration is necessary because some aspects of each of these men's viewpoints are quite different from the stereotypes that have caricatured their images. Thus, the following two chapters are concerned, in part, with describing the core of each man's derogations of religion. Once this description has been made, it will become evident that these two viewpoints have come to essentially the same conclusion about the same kind of religion. Albeit, each position used a different language system and came to this conclusion for seemingly different reasons. Once the conclusion has been established, the discussion will move to the next problem: the view of reality consciousness functioning in both positions. As stated in Chapter I, the theological assertions about man's nature must be allowed to direct the study; therefore, a critical analysis of Kierkegaard's position will be developed first.

CHAPTER

II

Pathological Religiousness: KIERKEGAARD

I. *The Masses*

"For me . . . this matter of the individual is the most decisive thing."[1] This is Kierkegaard's statement of the central focus of his authorship. It is generally well known that in Kierkegaard's understanding, "Christianity" in the Denmark of the nineteeth century had become the common property of "the masses." It was a group phenomenon that was perpetuated on the same grounds as any social institution. Those grounds Kierkegaard summed up in the expression: "In numbers there is power." In *Attack Upon "Christendom"* he gives this ironic account of the fallacy which distorted the religious situation:

The illusion of a Christian nation is due doubtless to the power which number exercises over the imagination. . . . They tell a ludicrous story about an innkeeper. . . . It is said that he sold his beer by the bottle for a cent less than he paid for it; and when a certain man said to him, "How does that balance the account? That means to spend money," he replied, "No, my friend, it's the big number that does it" — big number, that also in our time is the almighty power.[2]

To Kierkegaard the pathos of this religious situation was heightened by the capitulation of the clergy to the social standard of "power in numbers." In the specifically clerical rationalization of his day, the power of big numbers was an indication that "where the masses are, there too is truth." In his *Journal*, Kierkegaard writes:

I have often put myself in the parson's position; if crowds collected to hear him, if the church were not large enough to hold the great throng which waited outside, then all honor to him who is so gifted that he can be moved to talk with feeling, inspired by the idea that where there are many there must be truth, moved by the thought that there must be a little for everyone because there are many, and many who have a little of the truth are, surely, the truth: to me that would be impossible! [3]

It is only against this criticism of mass-minded Christianity that one can understand the basis and purpose of Kierkegaard's decisive concern for the individual. Underlying this concern was the view that the Christian religion as it was practiced by the group made each participant less Christian. It was only by separating oneself from the crowd that one could become one's true self.[4] Kierkegaard wrote:

The crowd is composed of individuals, but it must also be in the power of each one to be what he is: an individual; and no one, no one at all, no one whatsoever is prevented from being an individual unless he prevents himself – by becoming one of the masses.[5]

From the foregoing discussion it is evident how Søren Kierkegaard's concern for the individual grows out of his criticism of the church and its place in society.

With regard to the "Established order," which was the point of my polemic against the numerical, the crowd, etc., I have always done the very opposite of attacking it . . . but I have furnished what may be called a "corrective." [6]

It is evident that this corrective is based upon the following presuppositional views of the individual's relationship to the church in the " established order ": The church as a social unit is a less valid expression of reality than is the individual. Therefore, the negative implication is that a person who joins the church group is less " real " than he who stands apart from the church as a potential individual. The positive implication is that an individual becomes his true self not from joining the group but from discovering himself in his uniqueness over against the group.

Upon these premises Kierkegaard proceeded to the careful analysis of the manner in which the individual mind worked when it was under the influence of the group. The person whose mind is structured by the standards of the group and whose devotion is therefore to the objectification of truth is in the " Aesthetic Stage " of existence. It is to the subjective analysis of human thinking in the Aesthetic Stage that this discussion now turns.

II. *Aesthetic Dialectic*

Kierkegaard developed at considerable length many manifestations of the Aesthetic sphere of existence. A number of commentators have grouped these manifestations in two categories: the sensual and the speculative. However, it is not the concern of this section to develop categorical groupings into which the manifold forms of Aesthetic expression may be gathered. The concern here is, rather, to probe beneath such groupings to Kierkegaard's descriptions of the dynamics of consciousness that underlie all the manifold expressions of Aesthetic existence, however they may be grouped.

Kierkegaard employs two models to describe the psychic activity of consciousness: " dialectics " and " pathos."

When Kierkegaard writes of dialectics, he formulates *cognitive* constructs that are descripitve of the countervalence of forces in a given psychic act. When he writes of pathos, he describes how it *feels* to experience the particular dialectical balance of forces in question.

The major division in the *Postscript* (Kierkegaard's climactic work which stood at the center of his authorship [7]) lies between the " objective problem " and the " subjective problem." The objective problem concerns the truth of Christianity as an object of historical and philosophical knowledge. The subjective problem concerns the relationship of the subject himself to objective truth. Kierkegaard's repeated assertion is that there is a radical incommensurability between objective truth and the nature of the inquiring subject. The study of historical and philosophical truth can provide content for the inquirer's reflection, but the material per se cannot imbue the inquirer with a particular kind of attitude. Therefore, to make a purely objective inquiry, one must renounce a certain measure of oneself (i.e., a measure of subjective truth). By this line of reasoning, Kierkegaard sets up the two notions of truth in a subject-object polarity wherein lies the key to all his dialectical analyses of the individual's consciousness.

Kierkegaard suggests the following dialectical analysis of an objective inquiry. In order for a person to consider any material objectively, he must separate it from himself by reflection, which in the Aesthetic sphere of existence involves primarily the subject's capacity to form and relate concepts.[8] There is nothing surprising here; prior to any act of conception, one perceives sense data from the objects that constitute one's world. Conceptualization, then, is the subjective action upon this sense data enabling one to distinguish objects in general, specific objects, and parts of objects in their relations to the whole. The dialectic here is that in the subjective activity of forming perceptual data, consciousness has exercised its capacity to move into a relationship within and by itself, thereby gaining a conception.

Two aspects of consciousness are implied by the exercise of this capacity: (1) In the simple act of *perception* (i.e., receiving and organizing sense data), consciousness is not discernibly divided within itself. In this act a relationship of "immediacy" to the external world prevails to the exclusion of all other possible relationships to the environment. (2) The creation of a *concept* – and by implication the creation of a conscious difference between subject and object – requires (*a*) the negation of perceived data as being an intrinsic part of one's conscious awareness, and (*b*) the affirmation of that data as knowable apart from conscious awareness itself. From the standpoint of this subject-object analysis, consciousness does not supply its own content but rather is the interpreter of it.

This self-relatedness, in which one's *awareness* is by implication separable from the *content* of the awareness, is the psychic basis for the subject-object polarities, and in turn is the structural basis for the dialectical process of conception and reflection. It should be noted that the act of conception does not involve a dialectical tension between polarities of equal power. One's awareness is superior; it subjugates the perceived sense data and maintains contact with the external object only by retaining the data inwardly as the content of knowledge which is readily dismissable with a shift of attention.

It is evident from Kierkegaard's own awareness of the dialectic of conception (and possibly from the reader's own awareness of it in himself) that another dialectic is implicit in his knowledge of the first. This second dialectic reveals the cognitive character of dialectical analysis; for to become aware of the dialectic of cognition is to subordinate not only perceived sense data but also the entire previously established subject-object polarity to the status of a merely knowable – and therefore dismissable – object.

Though this may seem to develop into an infinite regression, it does not for the reason that the formal dialectical structure of the relationship between subject and object within reflective consciousness remains unchanged. The activity of reflection is repeated, and the knowable material is altered accordingly. The content of the object shifts with every successive act of thought, but there is no regression because only the two polarities remain: subject and object. Dialectically speaking, this is Kierkegaard's description of the Aesthetic sphere of existence: when the formal structure of a person's consciousness is a subject-object relationship, then he is in the Aesthetic Stage of existence.

Exacerbation of the structure by projecting it beyond the subject and then discovering it in the world's events was Hegel's essential preoccupation – and his failure, according to Kierkegaard. Any preoccupation with ideas as though they were discoverable things, or with things as though they were literally able to be transformed into ideas, was condemnable as a commission of what might be called the " Aesthetic fallacy."

Immediacy and the subject-object polarity together characterize the Aesthetic fallacy, but since a " new immediacy " comes to be a mark of " the Apostle," the relationship between " immediacy " and " objectivity " in Aesthetic existence should be explicated. Immediacy here is descriptive of the dependence of the subject-object dialectic upon sensual impressions gathered from the external world. This dependence implies that consciousness would be empty and void without the external world to supply its content. To this category one may relegate " Don Juan," " the Seducer," and their like. Yet he who speculates – as a metaphysician — prides himself on obtaining a knowledge that is precisely not evident in the sensual world. The metaphysician explains that the knowledge is in some way or other — depending upon which philosophical line he descends from — an enucleation of the true reality, the final and irreducible structure of being, behind or beyond this sensate world. In terms of Kierkegaard's notion of the formal structure of Aesthetic thought, it is simple enough to see how the speculative philosopher and such figures as " the Seducer " fall into the same error. Both have retained the same formal psychic structure for thought about life; the difference lies only in that the speculative philosopher has made the entire subject-object relationship of the Aesthete and the Seducer into an object for his own subjective consideration. By reifying the subject-object relationship, qua relationship, the philosopher is able to " discover " cognition as an object; it is an essentially nonempirical, imaginary creation of his own mind, but it makes him an observer of observers. He therefore thinks that he has moved to a higher plane of existence, but in terms of this dialectical analysis of consciousness he has merely exchanged one object for another.

III. *Aesthetic Pathos*

We turn now to the analysis of " pathos " in the Aesthetic Stage of existence. " Aesthetic pathos," writes Kierkegaard, " expresses itself in words, and may in its truth indicate that the individual leaves his real self in order to lose himself in the idea." [9]

Feeling in the Aesthetic Stage of existence is expressed directly by words. Kierkegaard uses " words " here in the broadest sense referring to symbols employed for the direct communication [10] of an idea. The term " language " is used by Kierkegaard in Volume I of *Either/Or* [11] to carry the same meaning. When " words " are the objectification of feeling, feeling has been translated into the formal subject-object structure of consciousness; a porous verbal structure has absorbed all genuine feeling and has been substituted for the feeling itself; " feeling " becomes a verbal symbol or is encased in words and becomes an object of knowledge.

If, for example, love is conceived Aesthetically, then the poet's *ideal* of love will be higher than anything that reality presents. Such poetic productivity is exemplary of the poet's mode of existence; his relationship to immediate experience is accidental. The feeling of the poet is translated into the ideas and images of which he becomes cognizant. His feeling is not a spontaneous reaction to any human experience, but, as representative of the Aesthetic Stage, his feeling is always captured, formed, and expressed in the subject-object dialectic of Aesthetic consciousness. The reality of an experience is, for the poet, merely an occasion, a point of departure, from which he goes emotionally and verbally in search of the " identity of the possible."

The example of the poet provides a further consideration: namely, the role of the imagination. The symbol-forming power of the imagination will assume great importance in the following chapters; but it is inserted here because in this context it makes its initial appearance in Kierkegaard's thought. " The pathos of the poet is . . . essentially imaginative pathos." [12] Formulating – that is, putting feeling in shareable form – is one decisive function of the imagination.

This Aesthetic characteristic of forming all feeling according to the subject-object dialectic means that feeling in itself is of less value than the idea of it, that is, than feeling translated into an image or concept. This, then, is Kierkegaard's answer to the question of how it feels to experience the dialectic of the Aesthetic sphere; it is, he says, the emotional state of "self-disinterestedness." The cognizance of feeling is separated from the inward experience of it, and the former is posited as more real. The more one becomes devoted to the Idea [13] the more Aesthetically determined one becomes. Feelings are accidental and misleading to the Aesthetic individual; therefore, there is no one passion most characteristic of this stage. It is, rather, the *reaction* to pathos that typifies it.

Thus, when the subject-object relationship formally describes the persistent structure of consciousness, when that relationship structures knowledge of the external world, and when no true private passions are permitted to intrude, then "communicable ideas" and "words" that express the crowd's opinion are able to control the mind fully. To such a mind, in which every known thing is objective, the determinative factor is quantity, i.e., the basis for deciding anything is the manner in which the relative quantity of objects tips the scales of the decision. To make a decision on the basis of quality requires subjective integrity apart from the power lent to an idea by its widespread espousal. It is upon this understanding of Aesthetic consciousness that Søren Kierkegaard bases his analysis of his contemporaries and formulates his ridicule, "Big number, that also in our time is the almighty power."

IV. *Summation: Aesthetic Existence*

Aesthetic-mindedness, then, has the central structure of a subject-object relationship. None of the forces that impinge upon such a rigid mold can alter its radical assertion of itself. However passionate one's feelings, they can be translated into words; however vigorous one's reflection upon his own reflection, there is no transcending the dichotomy of all truth into subject and object. The Aesthete, then, is a slave with two faces: if he seems to be enjoying the world, it is only because it does not really touch him; but if he seems to be transcending the world, it is because he has ascetically made an object of himself, the easier to be controlled by the weight of numbers and the crowd's opinions.[14]

By making this critical analysis of Aesthetic existence, Kierkegaard has implied the existence of a human reality that he repeatedly employs in order to pass judgment upon the facets of Aesthetic existence. This particular reality is still – for this discussion – undefined; yet it can be said that only the individual has access to it; and Aesthetic existence – far from leading one closer to that reality – seals one off from it.

Finally, it can be said that the image of feeling, the idea of oneself, and the ideational construct of the external world are, in themselves, destructive to this reality. This screen of imagery, ideas, and constructs is the very medium – the mind's manacles – by which one is enslaved through involvement in the crowd or in the church as a social institution.

V. *Dread and Despair*

Kierkegaard was not satisfied to name and describe this distortion of consciousness; the Aesthetic fallacy in religious practice was confronted, and its stubborn resistance to expurgation was exposed. The intransigency of Aesthetic-mindedness is due to the fact that it is not merely an error in thought, a misunderstanding; it is the persistent predominance of a fundamental structure of consciousness over human existence. From this premise Kierkegaard demonstrated that Aesthetic-mindedness is itself a state of despair, for there is no possibility that the subject-object dichotomy can correct itself. Even the knowledge that this state of mind is despair is not sufficient to alter the case, for the attempt to work one's way out of such an insistent frame of mind only deepens and intensifies the despair.

The following paragraphs delineate the lines of despair and dread as they appear in the "stages on life's way." The aim here will be to describe the way in which the sickness of Aesthetic-mindedness is redoubled and compounded by efforts to become "ethical" and "religious." The volumes which are of major significance for this discussion are *The Concept of Dread* and *The Sickness Unto Death.* It should be noted that "dread" is the English translation of *Angst,* the same German word that Freud used to designate "anxiety." Thus the translations create similarities and differences in wording that do not necessarily exist conceptually. The conceptual meaning of the words is a better basis for comparison; so, the discussion moves into the Kierkegaardian conceptualizations.

Dread

The concept of dread is first of all dialectical in that it is the product of endopsychic tension between opposites; as such, it is a matter of "ambiguity." The Aesthetic individual does not experience *Angst* except in an illusory, poetic, or imaginative form. If he "feels" it at all, he is imitating the feelings of others; he is not responding to internal, emotional stimuli. He is locked in relationship to an objective *image* of *Angst,* because he dare not know dread in any other mode. However, when one considers dread dialectically, it has, Kierkegaard said, "the characteristic ambiguity of psychology." "Dread," he wrote, "is a sympathetic antipathy and an antipathetic sympathy." [15] In its simplest form it is a "sweet feeling of apprehension" which deepens and darkens with the development of the personality through the stages on life's way. As Kierkegaard wrote:

Dread [as the "sweet feeling of apprehension"] has the same significance melancholy has at a far later point where freedom, after having passed through imperfect forms of its history, has to come to itself in a deeper sense.[16]

Dread, then, is a general term of which there are many shapes and forms, but at its inception it is a rather simple ambiguity of feeling.

The foregoing quotation, however, leads beyond the simple description of dread as an ambiguity of feeling into the larger dialectic of freedom. It is not by chance, or mere mention, that the notion of human freedom enters the discussion at this point, for it is woven almost inextricably into the discussion of dread. The first setting in which Kierkegaard discusses dread is the fall of Adam in the Biblical narrative. Here, Kierkegaard writes that the prohibition laid down by God to Adam "induces a state of dread," because "the prohibition awakens in him the possibility of freedom." This is the "alarming possibility of being able." [17] The relationship between dread and freedom is described as follows:

Dread is not a determinant of necessity, but neither is it of freedom; it is a trammelled freedom, where freedom is not free in itself but transmitted, not by necessity but in itself.[18]

By "necessity" Kierkegaard means the intellectual category that would be the opposite of freedom if freedom were to be intellectually construed. That freedom is not to be conceived as an intellectual category will become evident from the subsequent discussion.

But the fundamental question is, How does freedom trammel itself? And what is meant by "trammel" if it is not the insinuation of necessity into the experience of freedom?

An approach to these questions is made in the following description of dread:

Thus Dread is the dizziness of freedom which occurs when the spirit would posit the synthesis, and freedom then gazes down into its own possibility, grasping at finiteness to sustain itself. In this dizziness freedom succumbs.[19]

The clue to the differentiation of freedom lies in the phrase "when the spirit would posit the synthesis." Freedom grows dizzy when it sees itself as potentiality; dizziness is the epiphenomenal result of one's becoming conscious of the denial of reality implicit in the spirit's fantasy of stability. So the dizziness involves the simultaneous denial and affirmation of stability, and this dizziness is dread.

When the imaginative representation of the spirit is "grasped," i.e., the denial is laid aside and the "synthesis" believed as a concept is believed, then, in that act, "freedom succumbs," for the subject-object dichotomy is restored. But once freedom has succumbed, the state of dread no longer prevails. Thus, for Kierkegaard, dread or anxiety is the momentary or prolonged tension between the *image of the spirit* and the *denial of the spirit.* In itself dread does not represent a disorganization of the personality or a disassembling of the elements of freedom. Rather, it is the state of ambiguity that precedes, and perhaps hastens, but does not persist in the disorganization of the spirit and the downfall of freedom. It is, in essence, indicative that the spirit cannot be itself.

In this fashion, then, is freedom trammeled, but the deficient freedom of dread has both an *objective* and a *subjective* aspect. In the instance of Adam, the commandment of God came from beyond his mind, and his freedom, which was aroused by the creation of new possibility, caught an image of itself and was drawn into the ambiguity of dread. The commandment is the objective stimulus for the inducement of dread in the fall of Adam. In later generations the consequences of Adam's fall are accumulated, and the accumulation becomes the objective manifestation of illusory stability and therefore a basis for dread. These consequences are the precepts, deeds, and institutions of men, which become illusory images of potential stability. This, Kierkegaard called "objective dread."

In Adam's case there was no objective dread; but the nothing, the void, served to intensify the tension between the spirit and its image. In Adam's case the possibilities for the spirit were unlimited and also undefined. In later generations this "nothing" which Adam faced became "as it were more and more a something." By this "something" Kierkegaard does not mean a particular definable concept such as "sin," but, as suggested, he is referring here to the fact that, as generations follow one another, sensuousness (in the Aesthetic sense) takes on manifold forms in institutional life and in public images. Because of this multiplicity of sensuous representatives, the images in which the free spirit can see itself reflected are countlessly increased. The inevitable void that lies between the actual and the potential still remains; but the force of this potential, as the power of the imagination to conjure from public institutions an illusion of "freedom," is compounded by the generations. This understanding of objective dread underlies the Kierkegaardian concept of "the masses" and the influence of "number" which were referred to explicitly above.

By "subjective dread," Kierkegaard means the purely subjective aspects of the fundamental ambiguity of dread. In effect, subjective dread permits one to say, "*My* simultaneous affirmation and denial of the image of freedom." Thus, subjective dread was the same for later generations as it was for Adam, except that "in the later, individual dread is more reflective." It is such because of objective dread, but the personal, subjective import is the same.

Every individual in every generation recapitulates the Adamic struggle with dread whereby Adam's "fall" becomes one's *own*.

It remains to be seen what is the meaning and significance of an "imperfect form of freedom," as mentioned in the initial quotation above. Such a notion does not make sense if it is construed under an intellectual category. If it is so construed, its opposite is necessary, and any imperfect freedom would mean the encroachment of necessity upon the province of freedom. However, freedom and necessity as intellectual categories are mutually exclusive (except in Hegel's dialectic), so if there were any such encroachment, freedom would lose its meaning altogether. But Kierkegaard writes that freedom is not to be construed as an intellectual category; thus the opposite of freedom is not necessity. "No, the opposite of freedom is guilt. . . ." and "The relation of freedom to guilt is dread."[20] Kierkegaard writes:

> It is the supreme glory of freedom that it has only with itself to do, that it projects guilt in the possibility and also posits it by itself, and if guilt is posited actually, freedom still posits it by itself. If one does not give heed to this, then one has confounded freedom with something entirely different, with force.[21]

Kierkegaard's fundamental notion is that guilt is the consequence of the "fall" of freedom. In the hypothetical moment of freedom *prior* to the bestowal of guilt one creates not a self-image per se, but an image of the total self as blameworthy. The dizziness conjured by the simultaneous affirmation and denial of this imaginary condemnation is sustained as long as the guilt is held at a distance from the subject, i.e., as long as guilt is only potentially applicable to the self in the sense that the Aesthete knows himself to be guilty. *Once fallen* into a state of guilt, imperfect freedom may still Aesthetically push guilt from itself by positing it as an object or by fantasying the self into a never-never land beyond all appropriate condemnation. But all these machinations of dread finally crumble and succumb to the state of guilt; once enmeshed in guilt, freedom can, so to say, only flop helplessly within its entangling net.

Thus all dread is deficient freedom, but the decisive "imperfect form" is the illusory freedom of one who knows himself to be in a state of guilt. Guilt has an ultimacy in that it vividly exposes the sham of radical freedom and eliminates escapism, but more than that, it calls for a redemption of itself from bondage to Aesthetic thought on the one hand and to despair on the other. Thus guilt is the expression for the bondages of religiousness prior to redemption wherein the "supreme glory of freedom" is actual.

Despair

The discussion now turns to the analysis of despair which is the focus of Kierkegaard's concentrated attention in *Sickness Unto Death*.

There are two kinds of despair that are properly called "despair," and yet another that is not properly called "despair." Kierkegaard describes this last form of despair as "not being conscious of having a self." This form corresponds to the Aesthetic individual who partakes of "the common situation that the majority of men live without being thoroughly conscious that they are spiritual beings – and to this is referrable all the security, contentment with life, etc., etc., which precisely is despair." From Kierkegaard's standpoint this is despair because he posits that each individual has a self, and to be unaware of it is to be separated from it. To be separated from one's self and not to know it means that the possibility of freedom is remote. The individual's life is controlled by the influence of the masses; it is the masses who will tell him when he is guilty of a misdeed or immoral behavior. For him to project guilt in its possibility and posit it by itself is not possible except as an act of dread. Because of the remoteness of freedom for such an individual, Kierkegaard refers to his situation as desperate. He has fallen under the images of "the masses" and his conformity is fixed. However, because he is not aware of the bonds that enmesh him, it is not really proper to call his state "despair," for despair has to do with the sickness of the spirit on a level where the spirit can observe itself.

Another form of despair ("properly called") is "despair at not willing to be oneself."[22] Though there is an implied defiance in this form, Kierkegaard calls it the "despair of weakness." Its essence is not willing to be a self or willing to be another than oneself. Though it has many facets, the impression of despair is perpetrated within consciousness by willful denial of freedom or the refusal of an individual to accept himself. He may refuse to accept himself by sheer negation, in which case he implies a moral image by which he is measuring himself. Or he may affirm another ideal self as a method for denying himself, and again a moral image is imposed upon consciousness. This despairing individual makes the assumption that it is of no avail to imagine freedom, for it can never be a reality for him; even if it could be, it would not be sufficient because of certain unalterable – perhaps basic physical – deficiencies which freedom or "spirit" would not change. In this version of despair one becomes a chronic "loser."

The other form of despair ("properly called") is more manly and involves more consciousness in the sense that it is based upon the dialectical reaction to the "despair of weakness." Kierkegaard writes:

If despair thus becomes conscious of the reason why it does not want to be itself, then the case is altered, then defiance is present, for then it is precisely because of this a man is despairingly determined to be himself.[23]

In this form of despair the self hypothesizes that it is its own lord and master; and, says Kierkegaard:

Precisely this is despair. . . . By closer inspection one easily ascertains that this ruler is a king without a country, he rules really over nothing; his condition, his dominion, is subjected to the dialectic that every instant revolution is legitimate. For in the last resort this depends arbitrarily upon the self. . . . The self wants to enjoy the entire satisfaction of making itself into itself, of developing itself, of being itself; it wants to have the honor of this poetical, this masterly plan according to which it has understood itself. And yet in the last resort it is a riddle how it understands itself; just . . . when it seems to be nearest to having the fabric finished it can arbitrarily resolve the whole thing into nothing.[24]

It is evident that the " despair of weakness " presupposes some inkling of this last form in order to attempt not to be itself, but this despair creates compulsive " winners."

All despair is based upon the fact that " the self cannot of itself attain and remain in equilibrium and rest by itself." [25] The basic formula for all despair is

a disrelationship in a relation which relates itself to its own self and is constituted by another, so that the disrelationship in that self-relation reflects itself infinitely in the relation to the Power which constituted it.[26]

In order to clarify this description of despair it must be compared to its opposite.

As Walter Lowrie's footnote [27] indicates, his translation of this work is very literal, and hence the sense of it is somewhat obscured by the loss of nuances in the Danish which cannot be rendered into English. However, Lowrie has suggested that the following paraphrase of Kierkegaard's final formulation of the *absence* of despair correctly represents the intended meaning:

By relating itself to its own self and by maintaining its identity, the self has its clarified formulation in the Power which established it.

Comparison of the formulations indicates that despair subsists at the decisive point of " the relation " of the self to " the Power which constituted it." The substantive meaning is that the self inevitably relates itself to itself, but in despair this relation is caught in an image and envisioned falsely as a reflection of the eternal; in the absence of despair the relationship knows itself to be finite and happily reflects upon itself as the self alone without an image of the eternal. The latter form of self-relatedness is precisely the correct manifestation of the " given " situation, i.e., the self is constituted by a " Power."

The methodological point is that Kierkegaard is not concerned with a once-and-for-all categorical definition of the self, nor is he pursuing an analysis of " Power " per se; rather, he is concerned with the way in which the self understands itself. His mode of discourse is not ontological or metaphysical, but dynamic and experiential. What is expressed in Kierkegaard's analyses and pointed up by this comparison is his critical interest in the sharp contrast between the " how " of despair and the " how " of the proclamation.

Thus, despair involves not only a misconstruction of the eternal, but also a failure of the self to recognize that it is not self-constituting, but constituted by another. In despair the self-relation is " reflected infinitely " in relation to the Power that constituted it in that the self, in relation to itself, can go on infinitely imagining itself as something new, devastating old self-images and conjuring new ones. However, as such self-reflection goes on infinitely, the nature of the Power in relation to the self remains obscured behind "fantastic" notions of an inward "eternal." Since no compounding of self-images brings one into a unified relatedness with the "eternal" (such relatedness would be impossible, since the inward eternal is fantasy), despair is thereby compounded correlatively.

Despair, then, may be related to dread as a condition is related to an anticipation. Both involve a tension between the self and a self-image. But dread is the anticipation of falling under the domination of a moral (or any other) image *before* the domination is actually effected, or reconstituted; despair is the condition whereby one can never, by taking thought, emerge from the sea of *infinite possibilities* that surround the self or from a *specific pattern* of images such as Kierkegaard summed up as "the masses." Dread, in its first aspect, is the expression of the rudimentary freedom to *deny;* one can, therefore, deny his condition of despair. But every *positive* affirmation – its second aspect – which is posited by dread is distorted, reflecting the disrelationship of despair. Thus, dread always anticipates its own demise, but by means of denial, an imperfect form of freedom, it sustains itself at least momentarily. Dread, unlike Aesthetic existence, does not deny by turning its back; rather, it denies the condition to its face. This is both its strength and downfall; for the condition is more profound and eventually determinative.

Conclusion

The particularly unique aspect of Kierkegaard's analysis of religious pathology is its strict use of the subject-object dichotomy. As described, the "Ethical Stage" of existence comes into being when one becomes despairingly — not contentedly — conscious of his bondage to this particular pattern of being in the world, and, by dint of will, he attempts to remake himself after his image of what he ought to be. This is the ethical thing to do, but the dichotomy persists, making every effort into an object; and, thereby, surreptitiously, Aesthetic-mindedness is restored, but now it is flying ethical colors. The stage called " Religiousness A " appears when, in despair, one redoubles his efforts to break from the Aesthetic fallacy. He withdraws utterly from the external world, and flings himself inward toward the " eternal." But this attempt to break with all objectivity fails because the internal vision of the " eternal " is also an object for consciousness. Thus, the dichotomy restores itself even in religiousness. The kernel of religious pathology is the persistence of the dichotomy against one's despair both in it and of it.

However, the dichotomy must not be taken in a strictly intellectual sense; to speak, as some do, of Kierkegaard as anti-intellectual is a misconstruction born out of superficiality. The phenomenon being spoken of here is the cleavage of consciousness into subject and object, whether one is conceiving an idea, introspecting his last thought, or merely observing his own body in action. The self-destructive aspect of this dichotomy is that because of its control over the individual, he is always partially unreal in that he is not totally in his existence. His experience is always divided by the dichotomy. Once he perceives himself as unreal in this sense, then the reality of the dichotomy, i.e., its necessary presence as the basis of reason, becomes unbearable. Every new resolution of the problem is immediately caught, reflected, and rejected as another illusion in the service of the dichotomy.

The result is that one becomes suffused with the sense of his own weakness, his badness, and ultimately his guilt. He despairs because he is bereft of self-knowledge, and he has destroyed every illusion to the contrary, down to the very last, which is the subject-object division of his own psyche. This last insists about itself that it is an illusion, but it refuses to depart in peace. At this point, despair has reached its nadir and expresses itself in total guilt.

The movement of the psyche under the burden of this pathology is always toward some justification for its weakness, some relief from guilt at having been created in this fashion. Thus, Kierkegaard describes a reversion to the Creator as the author of the human condition, and to Adam, as the human father of mankind, for some relief from the blame. But the dichotomy is relentless; subjective dread is unmitigated by these considerations and eventually, in the state of Religiousness A, guilt becomes all the more intense because of one's having been created under the aegis of the Divine.

Thus, Aesthetic existence and the subjective struggle to destroy it encompass the forms of pathological religiousness. The profound observation that Kierkegaard made – which is both theological and psychological – was that the everyday condition of Aesthetic-mindedness is fundamentally self-destructive. Unrecognized, it emasculates the existence of the individual, making him a functionary for the masses. Recognized, it creates and sustains an emotional condition that cramps its own functioning to the point of no account.

This is the central thrust of Kierkegaard's analysis. It is plainly phenomenological and ultimately directed toward an answer to the question: How does one come fully into the existence of the present?

CHAPTER

III

Pathological Religiousness: THE FREUDIAN DIMENSION I

The plan of this chapter is twofold: (1) to present Freud's studies of religion as comprehensively as possible while concentrating on those aspects of pathological religiousness which directly illuminate the phenomena Kierkegaard described; (2) to arrive at a reasonably definitive statement of the nature of pathological religiousness representing a correlation of insights expressed by Kierkegaard and Freud respectively. Thus, although Freud's work focuses the analyses of this chapter, the selection of the material presented here reflects the presentation of Kierkegaard's views in the foregoing chapter.

The Two Analogies

Probably the earliest clear-cut statement in which Freud declares his position upon the general subject of religion is to be found in his *Psychopathology of Everyday Life* (1901).

I believe [in fact] that a large part of the mythological view of the world, which extends a long way into the most modern religions, is nothing but psychology projected into the external world. The obscure recognition (the endopsychic perception, as it were) of psychical factors and relations in the unconscious is mirrored – it is difficult to express it in other terms, and here the analogy with paranoia must come to our aid – in the construction of a supernatural reality, which is destined to be changed back once more by science into the psychology of the unconscious. One could venture to explain in this way the myths of paradise and the fall man, of God, of good and evil, of immortality, and so on, and to transform metaphysics into metapsychology.[1]

In this quotation lie the fundamental assumptions of Freud's later more fully developed interpretation of religion and of the method which he employed in making it.

Freud has used both an explicit and implicit analogy in this statement which, when taken together, are the double root of his derogating analyses of religion. The *explicit* analogy compares religious behavior with the pathology of paranoia in which there is an artificial creation of a supernatural reality. This particular analogy has its bases in two other Freudian notions: the distinction between conscious and unconscious, and the mechanism of projection. In order for the analogy to work, there must be a psychic unconscious – a sort of basement workshop in the psyche – in which an ego-alien reality can be created; also there must be a mechanism of projection in order to get that ego-alien reality established at some point outside oneself. By developing the implications of these two notions, Freud expected to reduce metaphysics to metapsychology; that task is only plausible because his presupposition of a sharp distinction between conscious and unconscious retains the necessary factor of a nonconscious reality – whether it is located in the deeps of the mind or in the world beyond the mind.

Thus the real root of the analogy between religion and pathology is the analogy between conscious-unconscious and natural-supernatural. The mechanism of projection not only accounts for the " out thereness " of the supernatural, but also effectively reduces the religious side of the analogy to the psychic one. This is, of course, little more than the logical outcome of Freud's faith in the supremacy of psychic processes and his " nothing but " mode of reasoning. It will be pointed out in later chapters that some of the phenomena Freud observed went far beyond this rather mechanistic model for systematizing his findings.

This analogy is especially appropriate to Kierkegaard's analysis of the natural versus the supernatural, since his views of the Infinite and the Eternal have a definite psychic dimension. While Kierkegaard did not explicitly locate these aspects of the supernatural in an unconscious mind, he did describe in his dialectical analyses the way in which they were created by the imagination for intrapsychic awareness. Kierkegaard does not by any notion such as projection reduce the ontological status of Deity to the psychic awareness; but he does insist that one's *awareness* of the presence of Deity is a psychological phenomenon, not a bald " spiritual " encounter that is essentially unrelated to psychic life. Thus may Kierkegaard's analysis be compared to Freud's position. In contrast, Kierkegaard's position lacks first the clear-cut distinction between conscious and unconscious and, second, the knowledge of the dynamics of the unconscious; but, on the other hand, Kierkegaard did not make the philosophical error of uncritically reducing ontology to epistemology as Freud did.

The *implicit* analogy made in Freud's statement is that the mythological world view in organized religion is nothing other than psychological processes projected into the outer world. This is an analogy between the individual and the group, individual religious behavior and group religious behavior; it clearly supplements and supports the first by truncating criticism from historical and social sources. Though such an analogical method carries with it a certain lack of precision, it is nevertheless of considerable significance for the comparison of Freud's analysis with that of Kierkegaard.

Kierkegaard, of course, was as preoccupied with the individual as was Freud, but perhaps partly because Kierkegaard never developed the first analogy, he never went on fully to reduce group behavior to the internal dialectics of the individual. The "masses" for him were always a reality over against the individual. However, he was greatly concerned to demonstrate that the masses destroyed human uniqueness, reducing the individual to a mere unit. This position, which was developed in Chapter II, could – without distortion – be extended and brought into line with Freud's viewpoint. That is, social organization is detrimental when it flattens the internal dialectic of the individual into "a spiritless sense of security"; so, in this sense, Kierkegaard agrees with Freud that social disorganization can be deduced from personal disorganization,[2] apart from all social and historical considerations as such.

Freud's deficiency as a sociologist is obvious; moreover, it would be possible to call the application of this last analogy a projection upon society growing out of Freud's social anxiety. That is, in his fear of social condemnation, he projected a reality upon society that it does not have (by all canons of sociological theory and research) in order that he might "control" it more effectively. This anxiety, it could be argued, began with his being a Jew, and it was intensified first by his own Oedipal struggles and later by his public persecution for his theories. It is notable that refuting the second analogy would leave the first vulnerable on the grounds that, since each society determines its own norms, any socially well-established institution such as the church cannot by definition as an ancient and enduring social institution qualify as pathological.

However, the main point here is not to refute the analogies, but to utilize the insights to which they led Freud for the purpose of finding a keener delineation of religion as pathology in the *individual.* Moreover, whatever might be said of Freud in this regard could also be applied in a similar fashion to Kierkegaard. Neither is a sociologist, but one does not look to them for sociological insights; the discussion must merely qualify its evaluation of their judgments accordingly.

Obsessive Acts and Religious Practices

In January, 1907, Freud wrote *Obsessive Acts and Religious Practices,* which is his most definitive statement of the analogy between mental illness and religious behavior. In this work Freud gives his account of two women whose obsessional acts provide an illustrative basis for a series of conclusions about religious behavior. These conclusions are:

[a] The protestations of the pious that they know they are miserable sinners in their hearts correspond to the sense of guilt of the obsessional neurotic. . . .

[b] The pious observances (prayers and invocations, etc.) with which they begin every act of the day, and especially every unusual undertaking, seem to have the significance of defensive and protective measures.

[c] Deeper insight into the mechanism of the obsessional neurosis is gained when the primary factor underlying it is taken into account: this is always the repression of an impulse . . . which is inherent in the constitution of the person. . . . This state of things has some counterparts in the sphere of religious life as follows: the structure of a religion seems also to be founded on the suppression or renunciation of certain instinctual trends; these trends are not, however, as in neurosis exclusively components of the sexual instinct, but are egoistic, antisocial instincts.

[d] In view of these resemblances and analogies one might venture to regard obsessional neurosis as a pathological

> counterpart to the formation of a religion, to describe this neurosis as a private religious system, and religion as a universal obsessional neurosis.[3]

The procedure which is most evident in these conclusions is Freud's various uses of the analogies. In the first conclusion, the analogy is based on a similarity between a characteristic of the intrapsychic state of the obsessional neurotic and a characteristic of the intrapsychic state of the pious individual. The similarity is restricted to the sense of guilt. The second conclusion is based upon a similarity between characteristics of external behavior: "defensive and protective measures" are given a ritual form by both the pious and the neurotic. The third conclusion is analogical in terms of dynamics: the structure of a religion has the characteristic of the suppression of instincts similar to, but not identical with, the characteristically neurotic individual's suppression of instincts. However, the implicit analogy is that the group is but a projected enlargement of the individual. In the final conclusion, Freud considers primarily the corporate concept of religion and, through "resemblances and analogies," notes that religion seems to be both corporate and individual; but, of course, the corporate is distinctly pathological because it is understood by analogy to the neurotic individual.

In pursuing the relationship of this speculation to relevant Kierkegaardian views, a more precise analysis of neurosis is required. But some preliminary correlations may be cited. Taking the points in the reverse order, the implicit analogy is repeated, explicitly now, in this fourth point. We have already mentioned the large extent to which Kierkegaard agrees with the viewpoint of this analogy. The notable change in Freud's view is that now religion is likened not to paranoia but to obsessional neurosis. On this basis the first analogy, while remaining formally the same as above, deepens into some precise behavioral likenesses that approach more specifically Kierkegaard's analysis of religious sickness.

These likenesses concern first "the suppression of antisocial instincts." The antisocial aspect of Kierkegaard's individual, which is functionally analogous to Freud's view of antisocial instincts, is "despair." For Kierkegaard, "Despair is a negativity" in the sense that it negates the pleasant spiritless enjoyments of Aesthetic existence. Therefore, it is antisocial, since all social existence is Aesthetic. "Unconsciousness of it [despair] is a new negativity," in the sense that one may be in despair but not know it. It is this same functional analysis of the double negation which is behind Freud's assertion about antisocial instincts. For neither viewpoint does a double negation make a genuine positive affect; only the illusion of a socially acceptable disposition is created. In essence both agree that underneath conscious awareness each individual has strong antisocial tendencies which are given with his very nature. The chief difference in the viewpoints is that Freud understands the unconscious in its perseity as the locus of instinct, while Kierkegaard understands it in the cortical sense of conscious awareness which retrospectively discerns hitherto unrecognized factors (the elements of despair) that have been operative all along.

The notion of ritual observances of the pious are for Kierkegaard as well as for Freud directly linked to the double negation which creates social acceptability. The "twaddle" of the Sunday service and the paganizing of Christendom are in the final analysis drastic errors because they have educated Christians into becoming nothing more than a "rude and ignorant rabble," nothing more than Aesthetes. The specific connection between ritual behavior and the alleviation of unconscious, antisocial inclinations was analyzed by Kierkegaard in his little volume *Repetition*. Here he notes that repetition is not really possible in the Aesthetic realm of human behavior. " Firstness " in any act retains a quality of uniqueness which may be valued for its power to point up the individual to himself, provided the act becomes more than merely interesting. To desire a repetition in self-contentment with no pain attached is impossible. Thus, it must be deduced that the ritual repetitions of the pious are the perpetuation of a religious sickness. Any genuine repetition must also repeat the quality of " firstness "; it is, therefore, not possible for the Aesthete who must objectify everything to repeat it.

Freud's correlation between " sin " and a " sense of guilt " must in the light of the analogies adduced earlier be interpreted reductionistically: " sin " is but another name for the sense of guilt. For Kierkegaard, the correlation also exists, but for him guilt is an achievement derivative from, but not the equivalent of, " sin." The condition of sin issues most directly in the psychic phenomena of dread and despair. Guilt is not yet present in sin; but it is the consequence of a fully conscious recognition that consciousness must necessarily be bracketed on the one side by the subject-object dichotomy and on the other side by despair. The bracketed condition of consciousness is given the name " sin."

This brings us to the crux of the discussion. The psychic structure that creates the guilt of which Freud spoke is the superego together with its depersonalized manifestation in the adult individual, i.e., the ego ideal. This psychic structure must now be thoroughly explored before the Freudian contribution to this Christian understanding of sin can be stated. In order to do this the superego will be discussed first in itself and then in conjunction with the general development of Freud's religious thought.

The Superego

The separation and interaction within the ego which creates the internal experience of an observer and an observed, a controller and a controlled, is made possible, structurally speaking, by virtue of the relationship of the superego to the ego.[4]

Briefly, the superego is the heir of the Oedipus complex. In a simplified sense one solves this developmental problem first – from ages three to six – by identifying himself with the parent of the same sex. Through a process which culminates in this solution, the child has managed to establish internally a sense for the actuality of the parents' world. In effect, he takes them in. However, it should be noted, the " parents " which are internalized are usually the parents' respective ideals of themselves. An *identification* will not do for the adult world, so the solution must be reworked during the years of puberty. The experience that has been accumulated up to this point has continually differentiated the superego and at the same time depersonalized it through the inclusion of surrogate parents, selected parts of admired persons, general principles, and broad social expectations. This differentiated and depersonalized superego is called the ego ideal. Taken together, the superego and ego ideal supply the internal institution from which all one's reflective judgments of reality emerge. The point for the adolescent is that now, through this internalized accumulation and integration of normative experience, he is able to solve the Oedipal struggle not on the basis of an identification with the parent, but " on his own."

Freud understood the superego largely as a metapsychological construct. However, from what he first explicated in *Group Psychology and the Analysis of the Ego* (1921), and later in *The Ego and the Id* (1927), it is evident that the superego and the ego ideal are the agencies responsible for imposing feelings of "unbelief,"[5] and of "self-criticism" or "conscience," concerning any endopsychic agreement between conscious functions in relation to the environment and the primary demands of libidinal energy. To the extent that this self-observing capacity is itself controlled by parent – or surrogate parent – figures or principles introjected into the superego or ego ideal the entire process is unconscious and therefore a matter of metapsychology. In testing the reality of a belief, what the individual experiences consciously as the influences imposed from those structural regions is of the utmost significance. The relationship between conscious experience, feelings of "unbelief," and conscience will be developed in the following paragraphs under the category of freedom.[6]

Freedom

According to Freud, in making a "valid" test of reality, the individual not only *feels* that he is free to choose the "real," but in fact he is free. (The distinction indicated here is between the solipsistic sense of radical freedom which Freud derided as an illusion and freedom as a fact of consciousness based upon self-knowledge and an understanding of the concrete alternatives.) In the *Introductory Lectures on Psychoanalysis,* Freud writes about the restriction of "freedom" (not merely the "sense of freedom") in pathology. For instance, in reference to the development of obsessional neurosis he writes:

> All these things [manifestations of the neurosis] combine to bring about an ever-increasing indecisiveness, loss of energy and curtailment of freedom.[7]

Regarding freedom in the positive sense, Freud wrote in *The Ego and the Id* as follows:

Analysis does not set out to make pathological reactions impossible, but to give the patient's ego freedom to decide one way or the other.[8]

Freud's declaration of the criterion for consciousness is that it be free in this sense.

This does not solve the problem of Freud's criterion, nor is freedom now fully explained, but this lays the background for Robert Waelder's keen insight that the formal relationship of the superego/ego ideal to the ego is the " structure " of the mind by virtue of which man is " free." Expressing Freud's own point of view, he writes:

Freedom, then, in its most general sense is found in the existence of the super-ego, in that formal function of the superego in virtue of which man rises above himself and apprehends the world from without and beyond his immediate perceptions and biological needs.[9]

Internal validation of one's perception of himself and his world therefore is the product of " freedom." Feelings of unbelief and feelings of conscience are the indicators of the curtailment of freedom or of the imminent onset of such curtailment. By a shift of attention to the internal manifestations of the superego and the ego ideal, the conscious ego can gain a vantage point from which to validate " freely " its decisions about the environment and about its own internal organization.

The Loss of Freedom

Obviously the nucleus of pathology for Freud's thought consists in the loss of this freedom. In obsessional neurosis the freedom is destroyed by the insistent imposition of a sense of ought upon every act; no act is good enough, wise enough, or certain enough. The obsessional is never motivated by " free choice," but always by what he feels he must or ought to do. His actions are a type of expiation or atonement because incessantly the reality that has been institutionalized within him tells him he is guilty. In the delusions of paranoia – to which Freud also likened religious beliefs – the failure of the internal institution of reality is also evident. In such delusional thinking, one may perceive the world correctly, but he is unable to interpret it correctly. Since it is the superego/ego ideal structure that makes self-observation and self-interpretation possible, it is also this institution which is the source of delusional misinterpretation of reality. The paranoid type of delusional system is particularly preoccupied with interpretations indicating that the person is being blamed, persecuted, or degraded. Other familiar types include delusions of grandeur, of exaggerated self-reference, of somatic disability.

Clearly, there is in this exposition of the Freudian view of freedom and guilt as they appear in obsessional neurosis and paranoid delusional systems a distinct similarity to Kierkegaard's analysis of the dialetic between freedom and guilt. For Kierkegaard, the capacity to observe oneself is the basis of Aesthetic existence; the subject-object dichotomy is contingent upon this capacity, for it makes reflection possible. It is when one catches himself in the act of self-observation that the ambiguous anticipations of dread suffuse consciousness. Then, as one Aesthetically retreats from dread, he makes the observation that his consciousness is bracketed by the dichotomy and by despair. At this point he is faced with the alternative: guilt or freedom. If he returns to Aesthetic life, applying the subject-object dichotomy to his existence, he feels suffering and eventually guilt because he has violated the eros of reflective reason which is determined to exhaust all of existence in the dichotomy. If he forces himself into dread, then he experiences the dizziness of freedom, but in a moment he is guilty again. His choice was short-lived because dizziness forced finitude upon him; he clutched at stability and thereby restored his subject-object world view. His seemingly unalterable condition is now known to him and he despairs, but despair is not the product of this recognition; rather, despair is recognized as having been the condition all along.

Kierkegaard's view of freedom here is functionally analogous to Freud's view of illusory freedom, because both describe a radical, limitless phenomenon, the alternative to which is a relocation of awareness at some vantage point within consciousness. (This latter type of freedom, while not common in Freud's view, was the goal of therapy; it was a fully expanded consciousness. As we shall see in subsequent chapters, the same goal is envisioned by Kierkegaard in the "new immediacy" of "the Apostle." However, we must concentrate here on the phenomena of pathology.) By correlating Kierkegaard's views with Freud's, this analysis concludes that Kierkegaard's description of dread and despair is a study of the birth and failure of "radical freedom"; for Kierkegaard also this freedom is an illusion.

The rise of guilt out of the frustration of the eros of reflective reason is a dialectical description of guilt's origins. The more intense reasons of pathos derive from the motivation of seeking an "eternal happiness"; repeatedly one "leaps" into his dread on the assumption that his radical freedom should be grasped if he is to attain an eternal happiness. It is as one fails in this venture due to the bracketed nature of consciousness that he knows that the proper name for his condition is "sin," and his repeated failure to grasp the freedom his imagination holds out to him tells him of his "guilt." Because of his sin he has become guilty; he has striven for an "eternal happiness by unwittingly exercising an illusory freedom." When this state of affairs becomes known to him, the passion of his guilt has reached its nadir.

For Kierkegaard as well as for Freud, guilt and radical freedom are alternative means of deviation from true freedom. For both thinkers, true freedom and guilt have their locus in reflective consciousness. In the absence of true freedom, guilt is the natural, fundamental alternative for all self-reflection. To be sure, one may disguise his guilt even from himself in many ways; indeed, it is this effort which gives rise to the regressive fantasy or illusion of radical freedom, but the root of the matter is that one cannot know himself without seeing that he is guilty; nor can he escape from his guilt, for all his escapes are illusory. According to Kierkegaard, the fundamental underlying condition is despair; for Freud, the underlying condition is a deficient appropriation of reality through the incorporation of the "ideal" parental images. For both men, the symptoms of the condition are feelings of guilt and attempts to escape into illusory freedom, together with antisocial inclinations that lead to a ritualistic behavior pattern and a conformity that is essentially a ruse. The intensification of the condition of despair may lead to the exposure of one's antisocial inclinations and draw him into a private religious system. This intensification is essentially different only in the sense that now one faces his despair or guilt more or less in private; the actual patterns of psychic distress are the same.

Moreover, Kierkegaard and Freud agree that a break from the neurosis of the masses is a step toward a solution to this condition, and both agree that the value of such a severance is in forcing one to face the full intensity of his condition. However, individual isolation is not the final end in view.

The major difference between what Freud and Kierkegaard describe lies in the distinction between Freud's ontogenetic analysis of the superego and Kierkegaard's phenomenological analysis of despair. Their methodological differences may seem to have drawn them to different conclusions on distinct levels of analysis; so, in order that any correlation of viewpoints be not too hastily conceived, we must make a further analysis of obsessional neurosis as developed by Freud in order to evaluate the conclusions that have been reached thus far.

Manifestations of Neurosis

In his short paper entitled "The Loss of Reality in Neurosis and Psychosis,"[10] Freud distinguishes between neurosis and psychosis on the basis of their different relationships to reality. In the course of this discussion he develops a useful description of the relationship that the neurotic has with reality. He writes that, in neurosis, "the ego, in virtue of its allegiance to reality, suppresses a part of the id (the life of instinct)." The "suppressing" action of the ego is a conscious activity; so it may be said that consciousness integrates impulses from the external world by accepting and adopting the appropriate images, but it excludes the stimuli that are urged upon it from the primary process that underlies consciousness. Thus, at the onset of neurosis, consciousness is at the service of the external world to the exclusion of some particular portion of the internal impulses that are pressed upon it.

> The normal or "healthy" individual . . . denies reality as little as neurosis, but then, like psychosis, is concerned with effecting a change in it. This expedient normal attitude leads naturally to some active achievement in the outer world and is not content, like a psychosis, with establishing the alteration within itself.[11]

From this contrast with "healthy" behavior in which consciousness integrates stimuli both from internal forces and the external world, it is evident that neurotic denial of primary process impulses cannot go uncompensated. That is, if these inward impulses fail to become expressed in consciousness, they will attempt to substitute another reality that is compatible with their basic demands. Freud writes, "The way in which this becomes possible is through the world of phantasy." In neurosis, images that express the primary process impressions are presented to consciousness as symbolic realizations of the basic needs involved. Since the symbolic realizations require no change in the real (external) circumstances, they can be juxtaposed; they can be attached to the images of external reality in an almost trivial, inconsistent fashion, "like a children's game." Thus external reality is faced and accepted, but in addition it is given a "symbolic" dimension which is inconsistent with its character as reality. Thus Freud states that in neurosis there is both an avoidance of external reality (reality not faced without a symbolic aspect) and a substitute for reality.

Kierkegaard's ironic analysis of the poet whose fantasy reconstructs the world so as to set himself beyond the possibility of experiencing "repetition," beyond the possibility of experiencing true existence, reveals full awareness of this symbolic distortion of reality. Since the poet is the paradigm for fantastic religion, it is evident that Kierkegaard applied this understanding of symbolic falsification to religious practices as well.

The imperfect relationship between the images that Freud described involves the consequence not only of a symbolic external reality but also of an excess of energy released into the psyche. This excess is caused by the circumstance that no image is presented to consciousness which successfully integrates internal and external demands. The diffusion of excess energy is experienced as anxiety. Thus anxiety may be described here as a presentation (*Vorstellung*) that cannot be bound to or translated into an objective image; consequently, it cannot be known except in a diffuse form.

Freud's understanding of anxiety was quite definitely in terms of what the ego could experience. Though it may not always be the conscious ego that is anxious, anxiety does originate in the conscious ego and is subsequently repressed; so it can be consistently maintained that anxiety is an experience available to consciousness. Freud wrote:

> The ego is the actual seat of anxiety. Threatened by dangers from three directions, it develops the flight-reflex by withdrawing its own cathexis from the menacing perception or from the similarly regarded process in the id, and emitting it as anxiety. . . . What it is that ego fears from the external and from the libidinal danger cannot be specified; we know that the fear is of being overwhelmed or annihilated, but it cannot be grasped analytically.[12]

Obviously, to have regarded a perception and to have "similarly regarded a process in the id" is a series of "regarding" actions which can only be ascribed to consciousness. Though not all of the ego is conscious, this, nevertheless, is Freud's meaning when he writes, "Anxiety is an affective state which can of course be experienced only by the ego."[13]

In addition to describing anxiety as a conscious affective state, the foregoing discussion and quotations indicate that there are three basic types of anxiety depending upon which stimuli are imposed upon consciousness and then imperfectly imaged or incorporated into experience. These were: (1) reality anxiety, (2) instinctual anxiety, and (3) moral anxiety. These three were originally differentiated in Freud's writing entitled *Inhibition, Symptom and Anxiety* (1926), but in this writing the concept of anxiety as being seated in the ego is not fully developed.

Reality anxiety occurs when perceptual reality gives notice of an event which is "judged" to be dangerous; this is more aptly called "fear." *Instinctual anxiety* is the fear that the instincts will get out of control and overwhelm the person. *Moral anxiety* is fear of the conscience; it is the insistent imposition upon oneself of an evaluational standpoint or self-image and the failure of consciousness to move into any other than an evaluative state.

In the development of a neurosis it is apparent from Freud's point of view that anxiety is the experience that gives rise to neurotic symptom formation. Evidence for this is the following:

> If one prevents a patient from carrying out his washing ceremonial, he is thrown into an intolerable state of anxiety, against which his symptom has obviously protected him. And, indeed, it seems as though anxiety development is the earlier and symptom-formation the later of the two, as though the symptom-formation were created in order to prevent the outbreak of a state of anxiety.[14]

As was indicated in the foregoing discussion of the relationship between neurotic and psychotic experiences of perceptual reality, the symptom formation is directly connected to the preference that consciousness shows for any particular impressions or images. This consideration would lead to the much larger question of the choice of symptom or of illness, which is not within the purview of this discussion. It must suffice to say that Freud believed that this choice was unconsciously determined by the object choices of early childhood and the development of the Oedipal situation in adolescence. The particular symptom pattern which is of immediate significance for this discussion is that of the obsessional neurotic.

Evidently "despair," as Kierkegaard understood it, is functionally analogous to "anxiety" as Freud described it in obsessional neurosis. Anxiety, like despair, is the underlying condition that leads to the fantasies or illusions of freedom. Moreover, for reflective consciousness, anxiety or despair produces consciousness of guilt, but as both Kierkegaard and Freud assert, the underlying *condition* is anxiety or despair. Freud's differentiation between instinctual anxiety and moral anxiety is analogous to Kierkegaard's description of the differentiations of despair. On the other hand, despair may present such a frightful prospect in the destruction of one's social self that one despairs at being in despair and flees all the more fervently into Aesthetic life. On the other hand, one may defiantly engage his despair precisely because he would be guilty if he did not. Only eventually does he learn that he becomes guilty in the religious sense if he attempts to encounter despair face to face.

In Freud's analysis of obsessional neurosis, two special features emerge: doubt and compulsion. "The doubt corresponds to the patient's internal perception of his own indecision, which . . . takes possession of him in face of every intended action." [15] The phenomenon of anxiety is the persistent imposition of an emotional pattern upon conscious experience. In "doubt," the individual's self-observation makes him aware of his symbolization of reality and the concomitant dispersion of his energies. This combination of doubt and anxiety is the conscious source of inhibition; the individual cannot believe that any action he performs is real or sufficient; hence, compulsion arises.

There is a clear-cut functional analogy between Kierkegaard's view of "dread" and Freud's view of "doubt." Both are forms of ambivalence ("the ambiguity of psychology") involving denial. Both arise epiphenomenally as heightened awareness: on the one hand, awareness of the world as having been simultaneously symbolized and objectified, and, on the other, awareness of the inexorable presence of anxiety or despair. Moreover, both "doubt" and "dread" arise as alternatives to guilt, but then eventually succumb again to guilt. For both Freud and Kierkegaard, this pattern in the relationship between dread and despair (or doubt and anxiety) is a matter to be faced, and yet impossible to face on one's own. The compulsion which arises – whether religious, or private, or privately religious – represents this seemingly insoluble dilemma.

"The compulsion," writes Freud, "is an attempt at a compensation for the doubt and at a correction of the intolerable conditions of inhibition to which the doubt bears witness."[16] In relationship to doubt, compulsion is an internally induced breakdown of the self-observation position and the imposition of some definite thought or action. Thus is the hallucination or pathological motor image (such as ritual) formed. Compulsive action or thought takes place when the accumulation of anxiety becomes unbearable, and doubt and inhibition are no longer possible to sustain. Compulsion may, "by a sort of regression," be supplemented by obsessive thoughts. These thoughts are possible, says Freud, "because they constitute a kind of reconciliation, in the shape of a compromise, between the two antagonistic impulses."[17] Thus thought may be obsessive if it is performed to the end of reconciling antagonistic impulses after an accumulation of anxiety has become unbearable. This process takes place, however, only in thought; it is "regressive action," wrote Freud, in which thinking has replaced action. "An obsessive or compulsive thought is one whose function it is to represent an act regressively."[18] Such compulsive thought is undertaken with an expenditure of energy that is normally reserved for actions alone; hence the force of the thought is so unusually strong that it compels consciousness never to abandon it.

This compulsive thought pattern has two consequences: (1) the person becomes obsessed with understanding, for understanding becomes a substitute for doing (this was evidenced in Freud's case of the " Man with the Rats "[19]); (2) the compulsive person characteristically chooses indefinite or ambiguous wordings. Since the mixture of perceptual and fantasy reality is itself ambiguous, it could hardly have any verbal associations that were not equally dualistic in meaning.

Freud seems to have described precisely what Kierkegaard intended with regard to the intensification of subjectivity by means of the dialectic of inwardness. The subjective individual is very deeply distressed because he cannot understand even dialectically the limits of his own understanding. As a consequence, the ambiguity inherent in all dialectical thinking comes at least temporarily to his rescue. If he assumes that his thought can extricate him from his dilemma, he becomes a Hegelian, but in doing so he has Aesthetically " conquered " his doubt. More likely, his doubt will repeatedly force him into new dialectical struggles, compulsively driving his subjectivity even deeper. Thus, there is agreement between Freud and Kierkegaard as to the dynamic pattern which thinking traces in this particular type of pathology.

With the foregoing discussion of intense anxiety and the basic neurotic reactions of doubt and compulsion in act, thought, and ambiguous verbal associations, it is possible to understand a further technique of defense which Freud states is peculiar to obsessional neurosis and which has particular significance here. This is the technique of " isolation,"[20] employed " because of the high degree of tension due to the conflict that exists between his [the neurotic's] super-ego and his id."[21] By using this technique, one is enabled to deprive an image of its affect; the associative connections of the affect are suppressed or negated so that it remains as though isolated and is not expressed in consciousness. Thus, the basis of isolation is a splitting of affect and idea. Once this split is made, it becomes possible to negate the affect and accept the idea. The splitting process, according to Freud, takes place both at the conscious and at the preconscious level. In the first instance it is called suppression, and in the second, repression. When it takes place, it is interpreted retrospectively by the subject as that conscious " faculty," his " will."

This psychodynamic analysis of " will " suggests the human substrata for Kierkegaard's assertion that each " leap " up to, but not including the leap into Religiousness B, is an act of " will." If the will is not bona fide intentionality but the by-product of an illusory sense of freedom, then the very idea of it must be a cognitive interpretation of something quite different which happens unconsciously. " Isolation " is made possible by one's being able to take up a vantage point internally and reflect upon oneself; under the pressure of suffering or guilt, i.e., of not wanting to experience more of such pain, the individual leaps to a new level of understanding. But, of course, " the leap " presupposed the possibility that the new understanding was different from the past one, free from internal suffering or guilt. Such an assumption is impossible without the isolation of affect from idea; that is, when pain suffuses consciousness, only denial of it can give any grounds for assuming there is an intrapsychic haven into which one may leap. Assuming the isolation of affect from idea, one may make such a leap. Moreover, the leap can be attributed to a radical, illusory freedom because both are predicated upon ignorance of the fundamental condition of despair. Thus, from the Freudian standpoint such an effort of will is an illusion. From the Kierkegaardian standpoint the same illusion can be deduced. There is no fundamental disagreement on this point.

CHAPTER

IV

Pathological Religiousness: THE FREUDIAN DIMENSION II

The Delusional System

This final chapter on pathology must take up the rootedness of religious belief in the father complex. Since the analyses that bear upon this hypothesis are almost exclusively etiological and cultural-anthropological, there is less basis for a point-for-point correlation with Kierkegaard's views. However, these analyses have considerable significance for Kierkegaard's views because of the fundamental Freudian analogy stated in the previous chapter: conscious/unconscious is analogous to natural/supernatural. It is on this basis that Freud attempts to reduce religious belief systems to the metapsychology of delusional thinking. For purposes stated previously, Freud's reductionistic " nothing but " mode of reasoning must be considered a debatable aspect of his findings; as will become evident in the following paragraphs, the historical and anthropological bases of the findings are also debatable. The least dubious aspects of his metapsychology concern the ontogenetic development of psychic structure, its role in pathology, and the origins of psychopathology in family conflict. These aspects of his work will, therefore, have the greatest significance for what follows; the language and imagery of religious belief will be seen here as having its roots in family structures, and the appropriateness of religious thought will be measured against delusional thinking.

In 1910, Freud's study of Leonardo da Vinci led him to statements about the origins of religious belief. Here Freud develops more precisely the nature of the relationship between religiousness and neurosis by indicating that both have a common familial origin. This development may be summarized by the following conclusions which Freud drew from psychoanalysis and applied to the case of Leonardo da Vinci:

> [a] Psychoanalysis has made us familiar with the intimate connection between the father-complex and belief in God; it has shown us that a personal God is, psychologically, nothing other than an exalted Father. . . . Thus we recognize that the roots of the need for religion are in the parental complex.
>
> [b] The protection against neurotic illness, which religion vouchsafes to those who believe in it, is easily explained: it removes their parental complex, on which the sense of guilt in individuals – as well as in the whole human race – depends, and disposes of it, while the unbeliever has to grapple with the problem on his own.[1]

Again, as to the explicit analogy (Chapter III), it is obvious that the duality of Freud's view of the psyche has established a context in which God can reasonably be made analogous to the father and projected (or "exalted") beyond the individual himself. The advancement which this analysis makes over earlier ones is that now the "metaphysics" of the unconscious has become explicit: the paranoid-like delusional system of religious thought centers around the father who is also God, and he is the one before whom one is guilty when that guilt is religious. The unconscious is no longer a nameless region at the base of the mind; it is composed around a central human issue, the "father complex." The supernatural is no longer merely the " beyond," the " out there "; it is actually personified; it is the location of the heavenly father.[2]

In *Totem and Taboo,*[3] Freud developed his famous hypothesis about the racial origins of the parental problem that lies at the basis of religious need. His general conclusion was that religion had its beginnings in the *primordial* Oedipus complex. When the sons of the chieftain of the primeval horde banded together against their father and slew him, " this crime of liberation and the reactions to it had as their result the appearance of the first social ties, the basic moral restrictions and the oldest form of religion – totemism." [4]

By applying the psychoanalytic observations of psychoneurotic illness in children (in whom the primitive mind is reborn) to the practices of totemism, Freud drew the following conclusions:

[a] If the totem animal is the father, then the two principal ordinances of totemism, the two taboo prohibitions which constitute its core – not to kill the totem and not to have sexual relations with a woman of the same totem – coincide in their content with the two crimes of Œdipus, who killed his father and married his mother, as well as with the two primal wishes of children, the insufficient repression or the re-awakening of which forms the nucleus of perhaps every psychoneurosis.[5]

[b] The totemic system was, as it were, a covenant with their [i.e., the primal sons'] father, in which he promised them everything that a childish imagination may expect from a father – protection, care and indulgence – while on their side they undertook to respect his life . . . not to repeat the deed which had brought destruction on their real father.[6]

[c] Totemic religion arose from the filial sense of guilt, in an attempt to allay that feeling and to appease the father by deferred obedience to him.[7]

[d] All later religions are seen to be attempts at solving the

> same problem. . . . We find that the ambivalence implicit in the father-complex persists in totemism and in religions generally.[8]

The analogy basic to this analysis of the primal origins of religion is that between the cases of individual psychoneurotic illness in children and totemic practices of primitive people. Freud has noted that neurosis in children is the basic analogy for primitive religion, while neurosis in adults is the basic analogue for modern religious practices. Freud's method of analyzing religion as a group phenomenon continues to run true to form: from the analysis of the individual by analogy to the analysis of the group, and from pathological behavior by analogy to religious behavior.

Freud attempts to mitigate the weakness of the pure analogy by positing a kind of " collective mind " that establishes continuity between separate generations and makes it possible to neglect the " interruptions of mental acts caused by the extinction of the individual."

> Unless psychical processes were continued from one generation to another, if each generation were obliged to acquire its attitude to life anew, there would be . . . next to no development.[9]

This logic is, of course, not impeccable; but it is his best defense. This courageous but undemonstrable hypothesis serves to point out Freud's recognition of a fundamental, unanswered question in his view of the origin of religion, and to call attention to the fact that, in his own view, his analysis is based upon an analogical leap over a gap in history which had to be filled substantially. Nevertheless, it must be added that however questionable Freud's suggestion of a " common mind " may be, the validity of his analysis of religion does not depend upon it. It is cited here because it is one rather incomplete attempt by Freud to ground his analogically structured analysis in more solid psychic bedrock. This rather abortive hypothesis heightens one's awareness of the conviction with which Freud employed analogical thinking: [10] not only does his analogical analysis make facile correlations between religion and pathology and pass over the distinction between group and individual, but it also seems to have maneuvered Freud himself into the position of having to posit and defend the notion of a "common mind." At this point, the "common mind" seems to be little more than a stopgap solution which will allow him to proceed with the development of his two analogies.

The Future of an Illusion

We turn now to Freud's classic description of the nature of religion in *The Future of an Illusion.* Because this little volume can presuppose the racial and psychic origins of religious belief as outlined above, it can carry Freud's thought to its logical outcome: religion is an illusion. The nucleus of the book is contained in the following:

> An illusion is not the same as an error, it is indeed not necessarily an error. . . . It is characteristic of the illusion that it is derived from men's wishes; in this respect it approaches the psychiatric delusion, but it is to be distinguished from this, quite apart from the more complicated structure of the latter. In the delusion we emphasize as essential the conflict with reality; the illusion need not be necessarily false, that is to say, unrealizable or incompatible with reality. . . . Thus we call a belief an illusion when wish-fulfilment is a prominent factor in its motivation, while disregarding its relation to reality, just as the illusion itself does.[11]

Having thus defined an illusion, Freud has made the way clear to work out his familiar analogy. This time the development of civilization is seen as analogous to the development of the human individual. As every child must pass through a more or less distinct phase of neurosis because he is unable to suppress by rational mental effort so many formerly repressed instinctual impulses, so, too, civilization in its need for religion is passing through an analogous stage in its development.

Thus religion would be the universal obsessional neurosis of humanity. . . . The abandoning of religion must take place with the fateful inexorability of a process of growth, and . . . we are just now in the middle of this phase of development.[12]

Freud takes as his task in this volume the attempt to break down the illusion of religion. Religion should not remain, for it only detains man at " home where he was so warm and comfortable." He will have to leave home and

confess his utter helplessness and his insignificant part in the working of the universe; he will have to confess that he is no longer the center of creation, no longer the object of the tender care of a benevolent providence. . . . This may be called "*education to reality*"; need I tell you that it is the sole aim of my book to draw attention to the necessity for this advance?[13]

Before concluding this analysis of Freud's metapsychological works, we must consider briefly Freud's final major contribution to the psychology of religion: *Moses and Monotheism.* Here Freud takes his analysis of religion in general to the study of the Jewish (and to some extent the Christian) religion in particular. This analysis is of concern here insofar as it makes some contributions to a better understanding of Freud's general theory of religious behavior.

In this volume, following his analysis of Judaism and Christianity, Freud made a significant contribution to his former theories about religion by describing the importance of the "return of the repressed." This concept was developed in part to account for the unique power and majesty of religious feeling. The psychoanalysis of individuals, including himself, taught Freud that the earliest impressions, received at a time when one is barely able to talk, manifest themselves later in an obsessive fashion, although those impressions themselves are not consciously remembered. The distinctive character of these elements which return from a state of repression lies in the extensive distortion they have undergone as compared with their original form.

Freud felt that the same must hold true for the earliest experiences of mankind. One result of this individual psychic process applied to the early experiences of man is the emergence of the conception of one great God. It must be recognized as a memory. It also has an obsessive quality; it simply must be believed. As far as its distortion goes, it may be called a delusion; insofar as it brings to light something from the past, it must be called truth.

Basing his thinking upon this understanding of how the repressed returns in the individual and in the race, Freud analyzed the power behind the impact of the religion of Moses. Following the murder of the first Moses, his religion was discarded and partly forgotten. It was only later that it forced itself upon the people as a tradition. The religion of Moses came to the people of later generations with the force of conviction because it was a return of the repressed. About this return of Mosaic religion in the guise of a tradition, Freud writes:

> I make the assumption that this process was the repetition of an earlier one. When Moses gave to his people the conception of an Only God it was not an altogether new idea, for it means the re-animation of primaeval experience in the human family that had long ago faded from the conscious memory of mankind.[14]

Freud's allusion here is, of course, to the slaying of the primal father. This primal patricide, together with the murder of Moses (a uniquely Freudian hypothesis), gave the return of the Mosaic religion the force of tradition.

In the same volume Freud develops an analysis of Christianity which depends, for any validity it may hold, upon the retention and the return of the repressed. Paul, a Roman Jew from Tarsus, seized upon the neurotic feeling of guilt. He traced it back to its primeval source, which he called original sin; it was a crime committed against God that could be expiated only through death. Freud writes:

> In reality this crime, deserving of death, could have been the murder of the Father who later was deified. The murderous deed itself, however, was not remembered; in its place stood the phantasy of expiation and that is why this phantasy could be welcomed in the form of a gospel of salvation.[15]

According to Paul, a son of God, innocent himself, had sacrificed himself — and had thereby taken over the guilt of the world. In Freud's view, it had to be a son, for the primal sin had been murder of the father. He took upon himself the sins of all men; their guilt he could take only because he symbolized the leader of the murderous primal horde. Such a leader is evidently identified in Freud's mind with the poetic young son who conjured the fantasy of the conquering hero, identified himself with it, and acted it out.[16] As Freud writes, "Here lies the conception of the hero — he who rebels against the Father and kills him in some guise or other." Freud likens Christ's innocent assumption of universal guilt to the "tragic guilt" of the hero in ancient Greek tragedy. Apparently Christ's innocence is a derivative of his status as hero and leader of the emancipated hordes. His guilt, on the other hand, is before God, the Father; for as leader he is guiltiest of all the sons. Thus Freud concludes:

The Mosaic religion had been a Father religion; Christianity became a Son religion. The old God, the Father, took second place; Christ, the Son, stood in His stead, just as in those dark times every son had longed to do.[17]

Such is the essential rationale of the Christian faith when it is understood from the standpoint of Freudian psychodynamics. In terms of the Freudian assumption, it can be said that this is the metapsychological essence of the "Christian neurosis." One is made a Christian as a result of his inherited primal history that is reactivated in his unconscious fantasy life, expressed in his own Oedipal situation, and projected through appropriate images by the forces of the primary process into a religious interpretation of his conscious experience.

Again in this volume the crux of the argument is an analogy between individual psychic processes and the corporate mass of believers. Freud posits a racial unconscious in support of this analogy, and upon the hypothetical grounds of this corporate memory, he makes his speculation about the origin of religious emotion. As had been indicated before, the truth of this analysis does not stand or fall on the basis of the analogy. It must only be stated that this technique of argument controls the discussion in *Moses and Monotheism* as surely as it does in the other volumes which have been examined here.

Furthermore, the "return of the repressed" provides some additional explanation for the distinction noted above between the projected father and the nature of the deity. If one adds to the myth of the hero the power generated by the return of the repressed, more of the grandeur and magnitude to God are at least considered and accounted for. It should be noted that none of the factors that Freud thought necessary to add to the "father complex" mitigate the force of the explicit analogy between pathology and religion; indeed, the additional considerations tend to make the analogy appear to be an actual correspondence in which there is an identity in terms of psychological functioning and merely a variation in imagery which distinguishes the religious neurosis from some other variety of pathology.

These studies in the etiology of the Judeo-Christian religious systems are of particular value for this discussion because of the implications they have for religious language. The fundamental notion may be stated as follows: because the parental figures – the father figure in particular – are the basis of the superego, and because some chronic or traumatic disjunction appears between this internal locus of reality and actual experience, the language which arises to deal with this problem is compensatory family language. Clearly, the language would not have to designate father, mother, and son specifically; it could merely refer to an originator, a punitive power, a benevolent power, a place secured for those who are obedient, and a method of punishment for those who are not. One may build such a system around the welfare state or around his place in a business firm, but the most likely locus for a religious delusion is in ecclesiastical groups where the language is already of the family type and the very structure of the beliefs and practices is designed to recognize and reconstitute family-type conflicts. Religious language is an illusion because it creates an intangible world in terms that fulfill one's wish to be part of family solidarity; what cannot be accomplished in the actual family is displaced upon the supernatural family and worked out there. Religious language is delusional because it interprets the entire cosmos and even ultimate meaning on these grounds. Thus, religious language is pathological in that consciousness is deceived into thinking that it is performing an act of religious significance, whereas, in fact, it is performing a symbolic manipulation of an unconscious conflict.

Since the major weight of Freud's argument rests on the analogy that exists between known pathological characteristics and religious behavior, it must be further deduced that religious language is characteristically pathological when it is rigidly resistant to change in spite of evidence to the contrary. Such religious language represents delusional certainty; but equally problematic is the chronic uncertainty, or doubt, characteristic of the obsessional. The latter condition frequently gives rise to the magical quality of some religious language whereby actual events are supposedly influenced by the utterance of certain words or phrases. Finally, it should be noted that religious language is pathological when it is insistent that a symbolized version of the environment is more real than the perceived version.

This same dilemma of language and belief was also analyzed extensively by Kierkegaard. The full exposition of Christian truths along the lines of a popularized version of the Hegelian system – which Kierkegaard (adopting Freud) would readily have seen as delusional – has the effect of covering despair and "misleading the people." He saw that the Christendom of his era had made a religious system out of the state and had interpreted the reality of human existence according to this delusional assumption. His invectives against Christendom insisted precisely in pointing out the fashion in which "large numbers," the bishop's office, the state church, and individual Christians conflicted with the reality of existence. It was true for Kierkegaard, as well as for Freud, that the more rigid and pat the system, the more delusional – or erroneous – it was, and consequently the less effect it could have upon correcting the neurosis or despair underlying it.

An apparent problem for Freud's analyses is that they have shifted back and forth between neurosis and paranoia (a form of psychosis in which the symptoms are confined to the development of a delusional system), and religious thought has been classified variously as an illusion and as a delusion. The point to note here is not that Freud used nosological categories inconsistently; rather, he used them flexibly, as indeed they must be used. The general conclusion must leave nosologic categorization as indeterminate as possible, since these categories are essentially fictions created for the sake of convenience.

Far more significant are the indications of religious pathology that have been developed through the correlation of the insights of Freud and Kierkegaard. The statements that follow will not attempt to repeat the detail of the chapter; rather, they will attempt to crystallize the major focuses of religious pathology as they have emerged from the foregoing discussions.

The Indications of Pathological Religiousness

1. The subjective basis of the pathology is a condition of *anxiety* or *despair* which affects all of behavior including language. This is how the pathology " seems " to the holder when he views it directly.

2. This fundamental condition creates and intensifies the *problems of objectification,* both of one's " self " and of the environment. Both the self and the environment are highly symbolized, and the symbolization never permits empirical existence more reality than its symbolic garb can convey. Moreover, this symbolization permits what " is " to be magically manipulated in fantasy.

3. The intrapsychic pain or tension created by the inability to bear how things " seem " to be (the anxiety or despair is too great) and the seemingly necessary falsification of what " is " lead to the creation of *illusory* views of the world or *delusional* interpretations of it. Both are attempts to find " meaning " in the pain or " a meaning " beyond the pain. Up to a point, the more intense the pain,

the greater is the motivation to find meaning and to tighten the reasoning of the rationalization.

4. If the language system is delusional, then it is "willed," and considerable affect is discharged by being isolated from particularly threatening ideas. This affect must be drained off through *ritualized action.* It may be religious, such as genuflecting or praying, or nonreligious, such as face-picking or hand-washing. If the religious world created is an illusion, it is quickly doubted; the doubt gives rise to despair, and a ritualistic pattern of handling the subjective discomfort is adopted.

5. The predominant, immediate motivation is expiation from *a sense of guilt.* One feels incessantly that things ought not to be what they "are"; how things "seem" is too disturbing; no "meaning" is fully adequate or accurate. For religious pathology, this is a world of "ought" and "will."

6. The overall implication is that *the group,* which is constituted for the purpose of engaging the members in a ritual service that is highly rationalized and designed to gain for the participants forgiveness for their guilt, in fact, does nothing to correct this pathology in those who suffer from it. Moreover, it instructs those who suffer from a sense of guilt in a method to avoid facing it and working it through. It might be argued that people become members of the church for precisely this purpose, but the answer would be that they are not in fact members of the group at all. If that particular group did not exist conveniently, some other might do as well; if no group were available, then a private religious system could be created. The ecclesiastical group sacralizes the pathology, but it does little or nothing to alter its course.

These marks of religious pathology are in Kierkegaard's view a fallacious response to the condition of sin; they constitute in Freud's view a particular pattern among others by which one avoids reality. The psychic condition, apart from the particular language that is used to describe it, is largely an understanding they hold in common. The most important difference lies not so much in respective languages that they have employed to analyze and describe it, as in their respective views of religious language as it is employed by one in whom this condition resides. Since the pathology has been described in terms of psychic functioning, the principal concern with the language of religious consciousness has been how it functioned in the overall dynamics of consciousness itself. The logical implication of the agreements stated above is that there exists a pattern of psychic functioning that is characteristic of pathological religiousness regardless of the language appearing in its symptoms. That pattern has been described above.

As already indicated, it is indeed possible – even likely – that the language of some organized religion will be used in the symptom formation. However, as long as personal psychic functioning creates the basis for the significance that language has for the individual – not vice versa, i.e., language does not create for the individual himself the basic significance of psychic functioning; language is essentially communal and objective, not basically personal – the logical possibility remains that there is a pattern of psychic functioning that uses religious language in a nonpathological fashion. Because Freud never comprehended religion apart from the analogies developed, he very rarely examined religious language independently from pathological functioning. Consequently, he could never grant this logical possibility to the great religious figures of history. He did, however, maintain a view of reality consciousness that he described in terms of psychic functioning apart from language-system considerations as such. Therefore, nonpathological psychic functioning utilizing sectarian language is an option logically present within the scope of his theoretical viewpoints.

Kierkegaard, in his viewpoint, held that the great religious figures maintained a view of reality for which their language was particularly appropriate. In the majority of people such language came to be used pathologically; but, in " the Apostle " a view of reality was expressed that differed decidedly from the pathological behavior previously described.

Comparison of Kierkegaard and Freud on this point leads to the search for an understanding of psychic functioning in what may be called " reality consciousness," and for the understanding of how religious language may relate to such functioning.

SECTION TWO

Reality Consciousness

In Kierkegaard's writings, "reality" is often interpreted in relation to an opposite such as "possibility," but because the term often has more than one "opposite" and because at times the term is used undialectically, as in speaking of "historical reality," its meaning is not always self-evident. That reality which is of critical importance in affirming religious experience is internally discovered and existential. As such, it has a "dialectical" and a "passionate" aspect and serves as the optimal reality by which all other "realities" are given their relative value for man.

In Freud's writings, that which is used to evaluate religious experience is one of a variety of notions about reality. He refers to "psychic reality," "external reality," and "reality principle," all of which have somewhat distinct connotations. However, the last notion – the "reality principle" – refers to a psychic balance in which an integration of the other two realities is achieved. This principle of balance is the dominant immanent principle of the nonpathological mind, and, as such, it is the criterion by which all experience, including religious experience, is evaluated.

The argument must now make a more exhaustive analysis of Kierkegaard's understanding of optimal reality and of Freud's "reality principle" in order that their respective standpoints can be fully explicated, compared on a common level of understanding, and correlated. While some of the considerations developed in Chapters II and III will recur here, the following discussion focuses not upon pathological factors, but upon the emergence of reality consciousness.

CHAPTER

V

Reality Becomes Conscious: KIERKEGAARD

In order to encompass Kierkegaard's long struggle to achieve a final clear-cut statement about the human aspect of religious reality, it will be necessary to work through briefly the stages of existence and to demonstrate the meaning of " reality " for each stage. This will be necessary because the future use of Kierkegaard's view of reality consciousness will presuppose the analysis of the stages by which an individual *becomes* " real " in the fullest sense.

In the *Concluding Unscientific Postscript,* as the discussion moves beyond the Aesthetic Stage of existence (discussed above in Chapter II), Kierkegaard takes up " the relation of the subject to the truth of Christianity." To move beyond the Aesthetic Stage is to avoid objectivity and to involve subjectivity in existence. A major premise in the following analysis is Kierkegaard's view of subjective thought.

Subjective thought puts everything in process and omits the result; partly because this belongs to him who has the way, and partly because as an existing individual he is constantly in the process of coming to be, which holds true of every human being who has not permitted himself to be deceived into becoming objective.[1]

In this passage Kierkegaard has stated his dynamic conception of the existence of the individual and of the world in which the individual is involved. To become " objective " is to enter the Aesthetic Stage which is marked by a static, subject-object dichotomy. However, in this " objective " stage one does not recognize himself as such. That is, one may have the capacity for reflective calculation, for laying plans in the sense, say, of " the Seducer." However, he does not recognize that the planner's existence is the inextricable source of the plan, but, more disastrously, he does not recognize that to be defined by or absorbed in one's plan is to be lost to one's self. This apparent contradiction is straightened out by the recognition that chronic objectivity does not preclude the " feeling " or illusion of being absorbed; it only precludes actual involvement in the reality of existence. In " The Diary of the Seducer " (the final essay in Vol. 1 of *Either/Or*) Kierkegaard develops the analogy between actual-seduction and being-a-real-self. In his derogation of the Aesthetic view of reality, he develops the Seducer's elaborate and subtle plan only to bring the matter to the conclusion that, in reality, nothing happened at all. The Seducer as exister became lost in his plan.

Only a heightened and intensified self-awareness can truly grasp the captivity of consciousness in the dichotomy and allow the individual to move into the stages " beyond " the Aesthetic. These subsequent stages are all approaches to reality through a deepened subjectivity. The discussion turns now to an analysis of the next stage of heightened self-awareness, which is " the Ethical."

In explicating his understanding of individual existence beyond the Aesthetic Stage, Kierkegaard took as one of his major presuppositions a proposition stated by Trendelenburg. He writes that the chief merit of Trendelenburg's thought consists among other things in having apprehended movement as the inexplicable presupposition and common factor of thinking and being, and as their continued reciprocity.[2]

It is because thought and being are both grounded in an *inexplicable* movement that thought cannot exhaust being as Hegel believed. As soon as thought attempts to grasp being, it translates being into the realm of " the possible " which separates it from real movement. Thus being loses its character when it becomes an object of thought. When the individual becomes aware of this propensity of thought to reduce being to an object, for example, to reduce an actual seduction to the thought of it, he is able to differentiate himself as subject from any objective knowledge of himself and to impose a sharp disjunction between subjective truth and objective awareness. At this point it is his option to become an existing individual at the Ethical Stage.

What, then, is an " existing individual "? " Existence separates, and holds the various moments of existence discretely apart." [3] So an existing individual is one in whom the moments of thought and being are held apart. To see precisely how this separation is maintained, the discussion must again take as its starting point the dialectical analysis of the Aesthetic Stage.

There it was said that as conscious awareness became cognitive, it divided and moved into a subject-object relationship with itself. This primary conscious act of cognition is an expression of the inexplicable presupposition of movement which Trendelenburg observed. The groundedness in movement of which Trendelenburg spoke becomes " visible " to consciousness in the act of self-objectification, when the Ethical Stage becomes a live option. To introspective awareness, the movement of the conscious mind must take place with respect to that which is not moving, or that which is not involved in the movement; otherwise it would not be recognizable as movement. This relativity of the phenomenon of movement is evident in the familiar experience of illusory motion as when the train next to yours pulls out of the station and you, in your eagerness to be on your way, assume the motion is your own simply because you can posit that the neighbor train is stationary. The analogue is that to catch one's thought " in motion " one must be able to posit a stationary entity against which its motion can be compared. The total absence of an internal, stationary entity is " dizziness " to which Kierkegaard points as descriptive of the state of mind that prevails in the transition from one stage to the next.

Moreover, since the polarities of the cognitive consciousness are divided in and by the movement which is observed, this division must take place not merely against a contrast to movement, but against a sustaining background of implicit unity. Otherwise, the individual could only assume a dualistic consciousness, and all dialectic would be eliminated.

This underlying unity is not altered by the movement of consciousness either with respect to cognition of external phenomena or with respect to self-objectification. The reason for this has been suggested above: the formal subject-object structure is not altered in the passage from cognition to self-objectification; hence the underlying unity also remains unaltered. In other words, to know oneself as perceiver and to know oneself as knower does not alter the formal psychic structure. The only difference is that in the second instance – self-objectification – the object content of consciousness is the subject-object relationship of cognition. Hence, movement becomes knowable and the unifying background is implied.

However, if this background is always to maintain its

identity as an undifferentiated unity, it cannot ever become an " object " of consciousness. It is that which is, by definition and by nature, not-consciousness; it is that to which the existence of consciousness is always negatively related. Kierkegaard's phenomenological observation is that this implicit unity vanishes like darkness before the searching light of the knowing mind, as if the light by its very nature could not explore it as darkness. It is *ubique et nusquam*. Kierkegaard has many, generally interchangeable, names for this inward apprehension which seems to haunt every subjective act. The *Unknown*, the *infinite*, and the *eternal* (all understood in immanence) – all have reference to this phenomenon in the mind of the man who seeks to become an existing individual. It is this inward Unknown which is Kierkegaard's ground for asserting that the subjective person understands the teleology of the " self " as a " synthesis of the infinite and the finite." [4]

The element of the Unknown enters into the dialectical analysis of the existing individual as a negation of every relationship that consciousness can establish with itself. In other words, its intrinsic and necessary negation of any conscious attempt to objectify it means, for consciousness, that any movement of consciousness – no matter how self-critical – will always be limited to the finite and formal structure of object and observer. The Unknown is substantively nothing other than the relentless inward witness to the fact that the inner man is greater than consciousness can comprehend. It is this Unknown which is the dialectical factor in keeping the moments of thought and being from merging into an object; it urges everything back into process by negating every result. For him who has become subjective, no unity of thought and being can escape the taunting reminder of the Unknown that all conceptualization is finite and limited to the subject-object structure of knowing; conscious thought, therefore, cannot exhaust being. One is thereby driven into a negative existence of despair which is true to the extent that despair cancels the eros of reason and exposes the gap between thought and being.

Kierkegaard's entire analysis of the stages beyond the Aesthetic asserts that one is motivated by his search for an " eternal happiness " and that such a happiness is achieved when the individual is " at one " with the Unknown which, in the Ethical Stage, is designated the " eternal " or " infinite." Since it is the Unknown (by whatever name) that keeps thought and being in a continuous dialectic and thereby maintains the individual's existence, it is evident that to be at the same time both an exister and " at one " with the Unknown would necessitate a contradiction in circumstances. That is, either the all-encompassing unity of an eternal happiness would swallow one's existence; or the dialectic of existence would make the unity of eternal happiness an impossibility. It is the struggle to resolve this contradictory set of circumstances which typifies the stages of life's way, and no resolution is achieved until the final stage, Religiousness B.

In the Ethical Stage, every effort to grasp the " eternal " merely restores the subject-object dichotomy, since the " eternal," the moment it is grasped, always becomes an object to satisfy the eros of reason, and correlatively true existence vanishes. The same is true of the next stage, Religiousness A. Here also every effort to achieve unity restores the subject-object structure of understanding. Both of these latter stages are distinct from the Aesthetic Stage in that the external world is radically disavowed. Truth is inward for the ethicist and the religionist; therefore, the " crowd " and the " idea " have an indirect effect upon them. The problem is that these later stages represent no definitive change in the functional patterns of consciousness; the subject-object pattern either forced the Unknown into an objective status, or consciousness fell condemned and negated by it.

The major psychic change that occurs in these latter stages is the generation of passion – the passion of guilt due to failure to achieve at-oneness with the Unknown. At the decisive moment when the guilt has reached its height of intensity by being measured against an eternal happiness and when the dizziness of dread seems able to be resolved only by the individual's slipping back into the falsifying subject-object structure of existence – at this moment the God-man is bestowed, and the Absolute Paradox sets the individual into a criterional state of consciousness.

The God-Man

In order that the dialectical analysis of Religiousness B may be explicated, the discussion will turn now to the *Philosophical Fragments* and the chapter entitled "The Absolute Paradox: A Metaphysical Crotchet." [5]

The major premise of the discussion in this chapter is the point made previously that cognitive awareness by its very nature repeatedly attempts to subdue whatever phenomenon may threaten its cognitive nature and to bring that phenomenon into the structure of cognition as an object of knowledge. If this characteristic of cognition may be understood as the essence of "reason," it will then become clear how Kierkegaard understood the relationship between "reason" and the "Unknown." In Religiousness A, reason – going beyond the Ethical dichotomy between subject and object – passionately engaged in the destruction of its own subject-object structure in order to conform its nature to the *ubique et nusquam* presence of the Unknown. The Unknown remaining true to its character vis-à-vis reason, responded dialectically – it presented itself in a form precisely opposite to that by which it had been apprehended by reason. In Paradoxical Religiousness the Unknown responds to reason by bestowing itself upon the total awareness in the Absolute Paradox of the God-man. In this bestowal, reason is not merely negated but transformed into a function subsidiary to total awareness.

The first element in the Absolute Paradox by which the Paradox opposes reason dialectically is: the eternal has become temporal without losing its identity. This is "the absurd," a contradiction (*contra rationem*), not merely a nonlogical superrational paradox (*super rationem*). The second element is: by becoming temporal, that is, by entering into likeness with the finite form of the individual, the eternal expresses itself as absolutely unlike the "eternal" which hitherto the individual has conceived inwardly. The third element is: by so revealing its nature, the eternal demonstrates that man's searching his inner depths for the true at-onement is "sin"; reason had been pursuing a relationship with the "eternal" which is an alternative logically exclusive of unity with the self-revealed eternal in the God-man. The fourth element of the Paradox is: by paradoxically demonstrating the absolute unlikeness between itself and "sin" (subjectivity) the eternal bestows itself upon consciousness in a nonrational sense, i.e., it establishes the negating relationship with reason that reason had sought for itself inwardly. Thus the eternal proposes "to do away with absolute unlikeness in absolute likeness."[6]

Transparency

Kierkegaard's most precise and well-balanced dialectical description of what happens to the mind in this bestowal of the Paradox is found in the introductory portion of *Sick-*

ness Unto Death. The quotation regarding the " synthesis of the infinite and the finite " (see note 4) concerned the nature of the self as " a relation relating itself to that which constituted the whole relation." The analysis continues as follows:

This formula (i.e. that the self is constituted by another) is the expression for the total dependence of the relation (the self namely), the expression for the fact that the self cannot of itself attain and remain in equilibrium and rest by itself, but only by relating itself to that Power which constituted the whole relation. . . . By relating itself to its own self and by willing to be itself the self is grounded transparently in the Power which posited it.[7]

The transparent grounding of the self in the Power that posits it is Kierkegaard's most succinct description of the human experience of reality. This experience is criterional for all others; it is toward this experience, or state of being, that all the stages of existence have been directed. It is the effect of Paradoxical Religiousness. Therefore, it is important that the subsequent discussion make a full explication of what is implied for consciousness in Kierkegaard's view of reality as it is described here.

Explication of this meaning of reality will begin with Kierkegaard's repeated descriptions of the relationship between Religiousness A and Paradoxical Religiousness as they are given in the *Concluding Unscientific Postscript:*

If the individual is paradoxically dialetic, every vestige of original immanence being annihilated and all connection cut off, the individual being brought to the utmost verge of existence, then we have the paradoxical religiousness.[8]

The religiousness A comprehends the contradiction as suffering in self-annihilation, although within immanence. . . . The paradoxical religiousness breaks with immanence and makes the fact of existing the absolute contradiction, not within immanence, but against immanence.[9]

In religiousness A there is no historical starting-point. The individual merely discovers in time that he must assume he is eternal. . . . In time the individual recollects that he is eternal. This contradiction lies exclusively within immanence. It is another thing when the historical is outside and remains outside, and the individual who was not eternal now becomes such, and so does not recollect what he is but becomes what he was not, becomes, be it observed, something which possesses the dialectic that as soon as it is, it must have been, for this is the dialectic of the eternal. This proposition inaccessible to thought is: that one can become eternal although one was not such.[10]

In [Religiousness] A, the fact of existing, my existence, is a moment within my eternal consciousness, . . . and is thus a lowlier thing which prevents me from being the infinitely higher thing I am. Conversely, in [Religiousness] B the fact of existing, although it is still a lowlier thing as it is paradoxically accentuated, is yet so much higher that only in existing do I become eternal, and consequently the thing of existing gives rise to a determinant which is infinitely higher than existence.[11]

In these dialectical statements certain themes persist with apparent consistency. In the first place, the sharp "breach" between Religiousness A and Religiousness B is substantially the *annihilation of all immanence.* The complex internal search for a unity with the immanent eternal is completely abrogated in Religiousness B. Reason's self-destruction for the sake of unity and an eternal happiness is eliminated. Thus the first contribution of the Paradox to "transparency" is the elimination of the reflective internalization which was dialectically stimulated by the Unknown. The introspective relatedness with the Unknown is abrogated by replacing the Unknown itself with the dialectical aspects of the Paradox. It should be noted that the substitution here is not merely the Paradox for the Unknown. Such an understanding would be an emasculation of the transforming impact that the Paradox has on the individual. The Paradox includes *both* the Unknown *and* the individual himself in a relatedness. When the Paradox bestows itself, the *relationship* to the Unknown is replaced by the *relationship* between God and man in the Paradox, and this relationship becomes the " self " of the individual.

The second effect of the Paradox to transparency is as follows: the *ubique et nusquam* presence of the Unknown was like a blackening inward shadow upon reason's persistent attempts to illuminate an image of the Divine, but the God-man is historical (outside, in time) and external to the self (outside, in space). Hence, in the search for an eternal happiness one's starting point need no longer be the " assumption " that he has the " eternal " with him.[12] It is evident that the effect of replacing the Unknown is to turn the individual's mind away from its search to control and to restructure itself, and to focus it upon a historical figure outside the individual himself. Since the historicity of this figure is actual, not symbolic, consciousness of concrete historical reality is validated generally. This second contribution of the Paradox in its validation of historical consciousness as a psychic function simultaneously establishes the external spatiotemporal environment as one valid determinant of consciousness.

In the Aesthetic Stage of existence, consciousness was turned outward to the external environment, but it had not passed through the stages of existence and been brought to the external environment through the paradoxical image of the God-man. The external, objectifiable worlds of sensation and speculation were the sole determinants of the individual's reality. In the Ethical Stage and Religiousness A, the dialectic of inwardness was darkening and deepening but was divorced from the external world. Hence, in no previous stage was there any intrinsic correlation between the complexities of the inner man and the surrounding environment of Aesthetic stimulation. The inner world was related to the environment by means of a distortion; the subject was objectified after the pattern of shareable knowledge. In this " new immediacy," [13] however, a transparency is accomplished whereby the inner man is neither denied for the sake of the social-sensual-speculative life, nor is inwardness reaffirmed at the expense of those dimensions of life and to the detriment of reason's own structure. Rather, in Paradoxical Religiousness, the internal man and the external environment interact in such a way as to establish the individual in a total reality, for which subject and object are artifacts of reason's structure, not the major premise of all knowledge. Reason itself has become a function – not the framer – of reality consciousness.

Transparency and Existence

This conclusion to the development of the " stages " leads back into the larger context of Kierkegaard's writings and to the discussion of " existence " and of " movement " which were previously described as the " realities " of the inner psychic realm. To describe reality consciousness in terms of these realities, it must first be recalled that existence was characterized as a human state in which the two " moments " of one's life – thought and being – are " separated and held discretely apart." Movement was described as " the inexplicable presupposition of thought and being." Because of reason's restless attempt to reduce being to an object of knowledge, it was only the dialectical affect of the Unknown, in turn effected by the movement of reason, that kept the moments of thought and being apart and hence held the individual in existence.

Now, in Religiousness B, the historical, categorical nature of the Paradox drives the decisive wedge between thought and being. The Paradox is the God-man whose nature is unthinkable but not unapproachable. His nature cannot be objectified, but he can enter into relationship with an individual by becoming the relationship between the individual and the eternal in psychic fact. His nature cannot be understood, but in relationship to it an individual existing in despair may have his existence transformed. The Paradox defies an individual's attempt to conceptualize being by defining the relationship between eternity and human being as unthinkable.

Eternity, of course, can be conceptualized even if it be as a dialectical opposite to one's conception of time or as an inward Infinite, present only as the negation of consciousness. What is unthinkable, unavailable to the human categories of understanding, is an actual unity between eternity and time. Yet, since this unity in the Paradox asserts that it *is,* namely, that it has *being,* it is impossible for one who believes the Paradox, i.e., for one in whom the relationship to eternity exists in psychic fact, to reduce being to thought. Thus, in relationship to the Paradox, thought is categorically incommensurate with being; yet both thought and being are affirmed. Kierkegaard writes:

Human understanding has vulgarly occupied itself with nothing but understanding, but if it would only take the trouble to understand itself, at the same time it would simply have to posit the Paradox. The Paradox is not a concession but a category, an ontological definition which expresses the relation between an Existing Cognitive Spirit and Eternal Truth.[14]

Thus, the existentential effect of the Paradox upon the moments of thought and being is the same as that of the

Unknown, but now individual existence – the dialectical consequence of relationship to the Paradox – has an objective, historical determinant.

The significance of this historical determinant for the understanding of the inexplicable movement which underlies thought and being is that movement is now evidently more than the dynamism that animates psychic life. It is a direct expression of the Power that maintains the totality of individual existence and that "constitutes the self."

This conclusion is derived from tracing Kierkegaard's thought through the following line of reasoning: If, by virtue of the Paradox, an individual may become transparently grounded in the Power that posits him as an existing self, and if one may understand his existence as the separation within himself of the moments of thought and being, and if movement is the inexplicable presupposition of both thought *and* being, then it may be concluded that the experience of movement is the direct psychic expression of the Power that posits the self.

To be sure, this may not seem to be a necessary logical relationship, for it is possible that Kierkegaard is referring to totally separate aspects of life in his use of "movement" and "Power"; but if this movement is not the psychic manifestation of Power, then it must have an independent existence. That, however, is not possible since movement is an inextricable part of the existing self, and the self was posited by that Power. That is, if movement is an independent, dynamistic element of the psyche, it was at least *posited* by the Power that posits the self. But when the self is an existing self, it is *transparently* grounded in the Power that posits it. Movement, understood as fundamental to human life, is the *sine qua non* of existentiality; therefore, if "transparent" may be taken quite literally as allowing perfect transmission with no distortion or refracting image,[15] it may be concluded that the movement which is the presupposition of the existing self is a direct expression of the Power that posits the relationship which is the self.

The meaning of the foregoing conclusion for understanding " transparency " as reality is as follows: transparency in the individual occurs when the Paradox, as the historical determinant of existentiality in the self, categorically eliminates a fixed unity of thought and being, and thereby makes psychic " movement " — the direct expression of the Power that posits the self — the cardinal aspect of psychic life. Transparency of the self at its greatest height allows a perfect congruence between the two sides of experience which consciousness separates, and between which consciousness mediates: (1) the Power that underlies the self, and (2) a historical determinant.

If in reality consciousness, thought, and being are held apart, then thought cannot consume being, but it must understand itself as tentative in its comprehension of objects and be certain only about the tentativeness of its own nature. Consequently, thought can become the instrument by which psychic movement and historical event can be related, because the dynamism of " movement " and the changeableness of the external environment — a fact that makes history only a possibility [16] — require a flexible instrument that is aware of its own limitations. So transparency is an inward event, or realization, in which objective — historical or environmental — events and psychic movement are in such excellent correlation and interaction that the function of the mediation of thought is to make itself periodically unnecessary. In moments of clearest insight the activity of thought upon the transparent correlation can only prove to be redundancy, affirming the unnecessary character of its activity. As will be noted later, it is only in the particular moment of one's transparency that thought is excessive and redundant; thought retains a very active role in grasping the environment and interpreting the historical aspects of the God-man. But transparency is not achieved by thought; transparency is that condition in which thought is reminded of its tentative nature and urged " to put everything in process." It is for Kierkegaard the " new " immediate reality experience.

If illusion may be characterized phenomenologically as a perception of a nonexistent reality, then, with the above understanding of reality in mind, the conclusions of Chapter II are confirmed: the inward " eternal " is an illusion accompanied by a delusional interpretation. By itself this immanent " eternal " has no part in reality whatsoever; it is condemned as false (" sin ") the moment the Paradox imposes its transforming effect. Though not a part of reality itself, the Unknown was a " torment of passion " available to reason only through what " the imagination may suggest (the monstrous, the ludicrous, etc.)." [17] Thus it was a goad for the passions of reason, for engendering the passions that support reason in its quest for a grasp of the " eternal."

The Passion of Joy

It is to the passions that underlie and support the Paradox and the reality experience which it effects, that the discussion now turns. Before being faced with the Paradox, reason, inspired by its pride and its lust for domination, sought to encompass all, including the " eternal." However, confronted by the Paradox, it is offended because the Paradox does not acquiesce to explanation. Reason asserts that the Paradox is absurd, but that, says Kierkegaard, is mere mimicry, since " the Paradox is the Paradox, *quia absurdum.*" Reason holds aloof from the Paradox and keeps to the probable, but all that reason has to say about the Paradox it has learned from the Paradox. However, says Kierkegaard, reason " would like to pose as the discoverer, making use of acoustic illusion." The acoustic illusion is the necessary passivity of reason before the category of the Paradox and the consequent necessity for all that is said by reason to be merely an echo of the category of Paradoxical Truth.

When the Reason says that it cannot get the Paradox into its head, it was not the Reason that made the discovery but the Paradox, which is so paradoxical as to declare the Reason a blockhead and a dunce, capable at the most of saying yes and no to the same thing.[18]

At this level of encounter, the reason always holds itself aloof, echoing the mockery of the Paradox.

It is when reason and the Paradox " encounter each other happily," when the pride of reason is set aside, that the Paradox bestows itself. This bestowal is received with a passion which Kierkegaard calls " faith." Most significantly, the bestowal of the Paradox is *not* an act of will; [19] the will does not push reason aside and assert the absurd, for, as may have been anticipated from the previous discussion, the bestowal of the Paradox brings about such a transformation in the " faithful " one that he himself bears happily the condition of reality consciousness. Thus, assertion of the will could hardly be the condition for the Paradox's bestowing itself.[20]

Absence of this will as the effective agency suggests that emotionally the bestowal of the Paradox and the realization of reality consciousness bring about a release of the dialectical tension between the passion to know and the essentially unknowable. Thus, Kierkegaard speaks of this event, " where the resistance of objective uncertainty only results in the release of the passionate certitude of faith." [21] Such a release was experienced by Kierkegaard himself in his hour of "indescribable joy" on May 19, 1838. He writes:

There is an indescribable joy which enkindles us as inexplicably as the apostle's outburst comes gratuitously: "Rejoice I say unto you, and again I say unto you rejoice." – Not a joy over this or that but the soul's mighty song, "with tongue and mouth from the bottom of the heart"; "I rejoice through my joy, in, at, with, over, by and with my joy" – a heavenly refrain, as it were, suddenly breaks off our other song; a joy which cools and refreshes us like a breath of wind, a wave of air, from the trade wind which blows from the plains of Mamre to the everlasting habitation.[22]

Such a release characterizes the outwardness of "the Apostle" in Kierkegaard's thinking.

The Apostle's . . . life is turned outward, employed in spreading Christianity throughout kingdoms and lands. . . . The direct relation is an Aesthetic relation (oriented outward), and to that extent lower – and yet as an exception it is higher for the Apostle. The paradox consists precisely in the fact that what counts as higher for an Apostle does not so count for others.[23]

For a "disciple at second hand," not in the historical setting with the God-man, this Apostolic outwardness which is "above" the Aesthetic existence is achieved only by passing through the stages of existence and then achieving the release of joy in the moment when reality consciousness emerges. In the development through the stages "the pressure is so great that the joy which comes (from the Paradox) cannot be taken as vain."[24]

The Concluding Definition

Reality consciousness vis-à-vis the thought of Kierkegaard may be defined as follows: It is that joyful state of existence in which one finds that the movement which underlies his thought and being so relate him to his external environment that he is capable of being independent of its categories, but at the same time capable of having, through his response to and understanding of the environment, a direct and effective interaction with it and its categories.[25]

This definition intentionally avoids the intrinsically theological and metaphysical considerations in Kierkegaard's understanding of reality in order that it may confine itself to the human experience of it.[26] However, this understanding of the Kierkegaardian reality, as the entire foregoing discussion has attempted to demonstrate, is not only consistent with those theological and metaphysical determinants, but also is that by which their misappropriation is criticized and pathological religiousness is detected.

CHAPTER

VI

Consciousness as Reality: FREUD

The two principles which Freud . . . established . . . he termed the "pleasure principle" and the "reality principle" respectively. . . . It was this distinction on which rests Freud's chief claim to fame: even his discovery of the unconscious is subordinate to it.[1]

These two principles are the immanent regulating principles of what Freud called the "primary" and "secondary" psychic systems. This major distinction, which Freud made by grouping all aspects of psychic functioning into two fundamental interacting systems, is the key to his understanding of human reality. It is from his interpretation of the interactions between these two systems that individual reality derived its theoretical meaning. The two governing principles of the systems take their definitions from Freud's understanding of the possibilities and limitations in the interactions between the two systems; hence these principles are immanent in that there are processes which conform to them, but they have no existence apart from those processes. In the following development of Freud's understanding of reality consciousness, the processes of interaction between the two major systems of psychic functioning will provide the dynamic context in which the principles of psychic life will be defined; to study the reality principle purely in the abstract, or to study it apart from the pleasure principle, would be to falsify its essentially immanent and dynamic character.

Reality in " Two Principles of Mental Functioning "

To begin with the core of Freud's thought on this subject, the discussion will concentrate in some detail upon his paper entitled " Formulations on the Two Principles of Mental Functioning,"[2] which Freud wrote between June, 1910, and January, 1911. The central significance of the paper for the theoretical development of Freud's thought is indicated by James Strachey.[3] Strachey writes that in this paper, it is

> as though Freud were bringing up for his own inspection, as it were, the fundamental hypotheses of an earlier period, and preparing them to serve as a basis for the major theoretical discussions which lay ahead in the immediate future.[4]

This pivotal study is foreshadowed primarily by Freud's " Project for a Scientific Psychology " written in 1895 but not published until 1950, and by ideas developed in Chapter VII of *The Interpretation of Dreams.* These foreshadowings will be referred to where there is sharp divergence in Freud's thought, or where an explanation of such origins will establish the theoretical perspective for understanding the later, more fully developed statements of the reality principle.

In this pivotal study on the two major principles of mental functioning, it is evident that Freud retains his earlier opinion that the pleasure-pain principle is the primary psychic principle.[5] It is only in relation to the frustration of the pleasure principle that the reality-principle can be understood. In *The Interpretation of Dreams,* Freud made the sharp distinction between " psychic reality " and " material reality." [6] "Psychic reality," particularly in reference to the unconscious, was understood as essentially a mystery but was available to consciousness in the inward "perception" of pleasure and pain, as these "perceptions" give qualitative determination to cognitive processes.[7] "Material reality" referred to the external world which Freud also asserted was essentially unknowable but known to consciousness as external reality through the reports of the sense organs.[8] The reality principle is developed by using these two earlier notions of reality as polar conceptions, and by understanding the principle developmentally as the eventual product of their interaction through the stages of human growth.

In the infant the primary processes, obedient to the pleasure principle, strive toward gaining pleasure; psychical activity seeks to avoid any event that might arouse unpleasure. The child's psychic activity in the strife to gain pleasure is described as moving from a state of rest into a state of disturbance (conflict with the environment) under the preemptory demands of internal needs. Freud writes:

> When this happened, whatever was thought of (wished for) was simply presented in a hallucinatory manner, just as . . . happens . . . with our dream-thoughts every night. It was only the non-occurrence of the expected satisfaction, the disappointment experienced, that led to the abandonment of this attempt at satisfaction by means of hallucination.[9]

This is Freud's description of the frustration of the pleasure principle and its activity, in which the reality principle has its origin.

This situation of frustration might be put succinctly, in terms of the language of *The Interpretation of Dreams,* as the conflict between "psychic reality" and "material reality." However, the nature of the conflict as it is described here must be carefully noted: the pleasure principle is first in conflict with the external world because satisfaction of the internal need is not immediately forthcoming. Hallucinatory activity is the attempt of the pleasure principle to resolve the conflict by means of its own resources, attributing " reality " to a mental image of the need as satisfied. This is the stage of conflict at which the reality principle emerges. When no satisfaction is gained from the hallucination, then

> the psychical apparatus has to decide to form a conception of the real circumstances in the external world and to endeavor to make a real alteration in them. A new principle of mental functioning was thus introduced; what was presented in the mind was no longer what was agreeable but what was real, even if it happened to be disagreeable.[10]

This is the genesis of the reality principle understood developmentally.

What comes to be operative in the adult mind as a " reality principle," whose automatic functioning is hardly noticed, is a product of the maturation of the interaction between the individual's " conception " of the external world and the pressure of the primary process operating under the direction of the pleasure principle. This " dynamic " understanding of reality is predominant in the earlier stages of the development of Freud's thought.

An important theoretical point to note here is that Freud's references above to a " conception " of the real circumstances are expressions of his fundamentally Kantian view that the external world is unknowable in its essence; one can, at best, formulate conceptions of it on the basis of reports from his sense organs.

It can be seen that thus far in the discussion of this paper, Freud's understanding of the reality principle also suggests an " economic " viewpoint (as well as a " dynamic" one), having to do with the relative apportionment of energy to the various processes of psychic behavior.[11] Insofar as that energy cathects objects as reported by the sense organs and is used to restrain the pressures of the pleasure principle for the purpose of establishing a relationship between the external world and the primary psychic system, it is psychic energy operating according to an immanent reality principle which is "economically" interpreted.

Moving on to complete the fundamentally "dynamic" views expressed in the "Two Principles of Mental Functioning," Freud states that conscious functioning is related to the primary and secondary processes in that the primary process, operating under the pleasure principle, unburdens the mental apparatus of accretions of stimuli through motor discharge. However, the action of thinking upon the operation of the pleasure principle is restraint upon motor discharge. Thinking is experimental acting accompanied by relatively small quantities of energy cathected and discharged (an "economic" consideration). If the unburdening of the mental apparatus takes place in relationship to a "belief" about external reality that is established by cognition and experimentally altered through thinking, then the discharge is accomplished under the control of the reality principle.

Thus it becomes evident that "the substitution of the reality principle for the pleasure principle implies no deposing of the pleasure principle but only a safe-guarding of it."[12] However, as conscious activity develops with maturity, increasingly more psychic energy is devoted to conscious relationships with the external environment, so the individual develops, as Freud states, "from a pleasure-ego to a reality-ego."

In conclusion, it is evident from the discussion of this brief paper that the reality principle may be defined as an endopsychic demand for agreement between the external world as it is perceived, conceptualized, judged, and/or reproduced [13] in consciousness, and the forces of the primary process which press toward the experience of pleasure and away from the experience of pain.

The Changing Concept of Psychic Energy

In order for this definition to gain the precision necessary for making any comparisons with the concepts of " movement " and " power " in Kierkegaard's writings, the concept of " force of the primary process " will have to be clarified and elucidated. It has been stated repeatedly that the primary process operates under the immanent direction of the pleasure-pain principle. It has been understood that these forces generally seek, with no regard to the external environment, to maximize pleasure experiences and minimize painful ones. This, however, says nothing about the meaning of the words " pleasure " and " pain," nor precisely what it is that goes about " seeking " pleasure and " avoiding " pain. The following paragraphs will outline the development of the libido theory in Freud's writings and its relationship to psychic pain and pleasure.[14] The subsequent investigation will, therefore, be conducted primarily according to the " economic " model of personality.

In Freud's earlier writings, pleasure and pain had an almost exclusively biological basis. In " The Project for a Scientific Psychology " (1895), pleasure is equated with " the experience of satisfaction " and described in the first instance as " internal change " or " discharge " (e.g., emotional expression, screaming, or vascular innervation). However, this is only a momentary experience and does not relieve the " state of urgency or wishing." Only removal of the external stimuli that is causing the sense of need by the release of quantities of energy in the interior of the body can permanently relieve the tension. When the external world is altered on behalf of the subject's need,

> he is in a position, by means of reflex contrivances, immediately to perform what is necessary in the interior of his body in order to remove the endrogenous stimuli. This total event then constitutes "an experience of satisfaction."[15]

Though much more technical neurological analyses could be given, the above should suffice to indicate the physicalistic understanding of pleasure that Freud maintained in his earliest writings. What was in 1895, in "The Project," a current or energy bound to the various interlocking systems of neurons became in 1900, in *The Interpretation of Dreams,* quantitative processes that are perceived inwardly as

> a *qualitative* series of pleasures and pains once they have reached consciousness after undergoing certain changes.[16]

"Certain changes" at the time when the "Project for a Scientific Psychology" was written would have referred to Freud's intricate analysis of "periodicy" and its effect upon neuronic excitation, turning that energy current from quantity into quality.[17] However, in *The Interpretation of Dreams,* these "certain changes" refer to qualitative determinations effected by the direct linkage between quantitative excitation which is felt as pleasure and/or pain, and verbal or visual memories. Freud's view here was that the verbal and pictorial images of dream life were resident in the unconscious and were produced as hallucinatory visions once the ego-control is withdrawn in sleep. This psychic regression to the activity of the primary process which typifies childhood is indicative of a fundamental Freudian theme: the primitive, the infant, and the dreaming mind are all controlled by the primary process which has the characteristic of expression — and often the satisfaction — of the pleasure principle through hallucinatory images.

This line of thought which typifies one of the major arguments of *The Interpretation of Dreams* yields the following very interesting notion, which suggests that by 1900 Freud's thought was already reaching out beyond the physicalistic frame of reference in which it had begun:

> The great respect with which the ancient peoples regarded dreams is based on a just piece of psychological divination. It is a homage paid to the unsubdued and indestructible element in the human soul, to the daemonic power which furnishes the dream-wish, and which we have found again in our unconscious.[18]

What lies beneath the qualitative experiences of pleasure and pain is, in its most elemental form, unavailable to immediate experience or to observation. Its nature, says Freud, is a matter of " deduction " from symbolic psychic expressions, among which the dream is the most significant and direct. By deduction from manifest dream content the latent meaning can be unfolded and the " deep-lying sources of excitation " can be discovered. *What is notable here is Freud's change of direction. In this volume he works from symbolic psychic expression backward to " excitation," whereas earlier he worked from a neurological basis forward to psychic expression.*

However, in Freud's thought, whatever the direction of the analysis, there is always an intermediate resource which is generally regarded as some form of energy or power. It is tied at one end to neurological excitation and at the other end to symbolic psychic expression, but it permeates the whole man, establishing the link between mind and body. The ancients divined its presence and thought of it as " the unsubdued and indestructible element in the human soul," but Freud recognized it in another form and established its residence in the metapsychological region of the unconscious.

In 1905, in *Three Contributions to a Theory of Sexuality,* Freud first made a differentiation in this energy quantum by dividing " libidinal " energy from other psychic energy. He then differentiated " libido " and arrived at the concept of " ego-libido."

The concept of libido, he writes, is

> a force of variable quantity by which processes and transformations in the spheres of sexual excitement can be measured. This libido we distinguished from the energy which is at the basis of the psychic processes in general as far as their special origin is concerned, and we thus attributed to it also a qualitative character. . . . We thus formulate for ourselves the concept of a *libido-quantum,* the psychic representative of which we designate as the *ego-libido.*[19]

Thus, " ego-libido " is the term Freud used to designate the power element of the personality whose particular function it was to activate the psychic functions that make up consciousness. " The narcissistic or ego-libido appears to us as the great reservoir from which all object cathexis is sent out, and into which it is again drawn back." [20] Since ego-libido is a derivative of the libido-quantum which has a sexual, somatic origin, it cannot be concluded that the ego-libido has an independent existence in the psyche. However, it is evident from Freud's distinction between " ego-libido " and " libido-quantum " that the bond between neurological excitation and psychic energy or power is loosening to the point where an equation between neurological activity and manifest psychic events is impossible.

In 1914, in *On Narcissism,* this relationship between the

function of ego-libido and libidinal energy is stated as follows:

Thus we form the idea of there being an original libidinal cathexis of the ego, from which some is later given off to objects, but which fundamentally persists and is related to the object-cathexes much as the body of an amoeba is related to the pseudopodia which it puts out.[21]

It is notable that Freud's use of the amoeba analogy illustrates his understanding of the organic relationship between the two libidinal energy sources and ego activity in relationship to the external world. However, in the same work, Freud loosened even further the libidinal energy from its biological moorings by positing the existence of "erotogenicity." He writes:

Now the familiar prototype of an organ that is painfully tender, that is in some way changed and that is not yet diseased in the ordinary sense, is the genital organ in its states of excitation. In that condition it becomes congested with blood, swollen and humected, and is the seat of a multiplicity of sensations. Let us now, taking any part of the body, describe its activity of sending sexually exciting stimuli to the mind as its "erotogenicity," and let us further reflect that the considerations on which our theory of sexuality was based have long accustomed us to the notion that certain other parts of the body – the "erotogenic" zones – may act as substitutes for the genitals and behave analogously to them. We have then only one more step to take. We can decide to regard erotogenicity as a general characteristic of all organs and may then speak of an increase or decrease of it in a particular part of the body. For every such change in the erotogenicity of the organs there might then be a parallel change of libidinal cathexis in the ego.[22]

The facile maneuvering of erotogenetic energy is the most definitive evidence thus far that Freud's libido theory is no longer dependent upon somatic correlations for its development. Erotogenicity, which is somatically rooted, described the special capacity of the libido-quantum to produce distinguishably different types of libido for the ego and to produce them with exactly the proper periodicity and quanity. The decisive point here is that now there are no observable neuronic or somatic events which actually cause the subtle maneuvering that psychic energy performs in its erotogenic activity; there is only a parallelism between somatic and psychic activity. It is evident here that the manifold and subtle expressions in mental phenomena have brought Freud to the point of positing particular types of somatic events, an erotogenic "charge," as it were, in all organs. Since these are not observable, Freud here reveals that he has now completely reversed his method: he finds somatic phenomena by deduction from psychic expressions.[23] From this point on, Freud becomes ever more definite in approaching an understanding of psychic energy from ego manifestations rather than from an analysis of the nervous system.

In 1920, Freud made his view of psychic energy explicit in *Beyond the Pleasure Principle:*

> We have arrived at these speculative assumptions in an attempt to describe and to account for the facts of daily observation in our field of study. . . . We would readily express our gratitude to any philosophical or psychological theory which was able to inform us of the meaning of the feelings of pleasure and unpleasure which act so imperatively upon us. But on this point we are, alas, offered nothing to our purpose. This is the most obscure and inaccessible region of the mind, and, since we cannot avoid contact with it, the least rigid hypothesis, it seems to me, will be the best. We have decided to relate pleasure and unpleasure to the quantity of excitation that is present in the mind but is not in any way "bound." [24]

The unbound nature of this underlying psychic energy is a major premise of this Freudian work which is so crucial for the development of his later theoretical positions. This essay posits a " death instinct " which, in its general tendency, seeks to return the human organism to its original inorganic state. In active psychic life it gives rise to conscious destructive and aggressive impulses as well as to the unconscious negative aspects in feelings of " ambivalence." [25]

The significance of this essay for the discussion here is twofold: first, it provides further evidence that, at this stage in his writing, Freud was able to interpret the energy that underlay all psychic activity quite apart from any specific neurological process. Second, it confirms the fundamental distinction between the two types of psychical energy: that which is " bound " and that which is " freely mobile." This view of energy is the theoretical basis for Freud's " economic " analyses of personality.

The second point is especially significant in that this distinction in Freud's understanding of psychic power corresponds to the distinction between conscious and unconscious energy or power. Excitation which is " bound " is expressed in the movement of consciousness, observable and describable quite apart from its generic roots in the undifferentiated libido or the libido quantum. Unbound psychic energy, subsisting in a freely mobile state, manifesting itself only in pain or pleasure, is – in its perseity – a metapsychological construction inaccessible to direct observation.

From the viewpoint of the power, or energy, of the mind, this distinction corresponds well with the distinction that was made above in Kierkegaard's writings between " movement " and " Power." Though it would be a *reductio ad absurdum* to make an equation between " Power " and " libido-quantum," it must be stated that the mobile energy quantum moving toward pleasure is that which invigorates the " joy " of release.[26] Consequently, the relation between unbound psychic energy and the work of the spirit in producing joy in the Christian sense is a direct one. Moreover, it is notable that "movement" in Kierkegaard's analysis is descriptive of an energy that is bound to, and lends the dynamic to, the dialectical processes of consciousness. On this general point, then, Freud and Kierkegaard have clearly observed the same phenomenon: a differentiation between two types of power or energy operating at distinctly different levels. At the shallower level, energy or power is resident within the processes of consciousness. At the deeper level, there are energy resources which, when they are released, may produce the experience of joy in which the two types of energy are fused. Freud's metapsychology of energy is, however, too broadly interpreted in terms of pleasure and pain to be *equated* with Kierkegaard's interpretation of the Power underlying the dialectics of consciousness. Yet in the phenomenology of the consciousness of joy, "Power" and "energy" are indistinguishable in their respective manifestations; "unbound" energy is essential to the consciousness of the presence of the Spirit, i.e., the "synthesis," but the metapsychology of such an energy quantum is to be clearly differentiated from the "metaphysics" of the Spirit.

Energy and the Pleasure Principle

If it can be concluded that for Freud a disembodied, freely mobile quantum of energy is seeking pleasure and avoiding pain, the question for this discussion now becomes: How are pleasure and pain linked with the specific aspects of ego activity? The answer to this question will require a clear understanding of pleasure and pain in terms of Freud's description of the primary and secondary processes.

In *On Narcissism,* Freud wrote in answer to the question of why damming up of libido in the ego should be experienced as " painful ":

There I shall content myself with the answer that " pain " is in general the expression of increased tension, and thus a quantity of the material event is, here as elsewhere, transformed into the quality of " pain " in the mind.[27]

If " tension " is the *sine qua non* for experiencing the psychic quality of pain, then all ego activity that exercises restraint over the unleashing of the psychic energy of the primary process is essentially painful. Furthermore, an increase in the quantity of tension corresponds to an increased intensity in the quality of pain. Conversely, pleasure is identified with the experience of a release of the psychic tension that restrains the activity of the primary process.[28]

In terms of what eventually evolved in Freud's understanding of psychic energy as it has been sketched above, it can be stated that the quality of ego activity is grounded upon the tension between ego-libido and the libido quantum. The psychic power of the individual alternates between division within (and against) itself and a unified release in which ego activity issues in a motor response to alter the external environment on behalf of the pleasure principle. This is to understand the power of the psyche as a mobile, highly differentiable force, not necessarily linked with any somatic sources, and capable of being divided against itself by becoming bound to the ego functions of the psyche.

With this understanding of the " economic " viewpoint, it is possible to reformulate Freud's concept of reality. The first part of the definition is the same as above, but in the following definition the latter part has been altered to include the now more complete understanding of " force ":

The reality principle is an endopsychic demand for agreement between the external world as it is perceived, conceptualized, judged, and/or reproduced in consciousness, and the power of the psyche which both energizes those conscious processes and at the same time demands, through the introduction of tension which is felt as mental "pain," the ultimate cooperation of those conscious processes in its own self-expression. When an individual himself becomes real, i.e., when the reality principle is the immanent law of his psychic nature, then he seeks pleasure in such a way that the power which underlies and energizes consciousness finds *valid expression* in the external world through the operation of conscious functions.

If it be granted that the earlier correlations regarding energy are sound, the notion of tension developed here is not fundamentally different from dialectical tension in Kierkegaard. It is precisely in the recognition and bearing of psychic tension that Kierkegaard's views of dialectic differ from Hegel's; for Kierkegaard, between "thesis" and "antithesis" there is painful tension which begets not a smooth transition to a higher synthesis, but consciousness of "despair." Thus tension is created in the breach between the two types of energy, and it is felt as painful. This is the first similarity to be noted. (Eventually a new thesis and antithesis emerge, but not on a higher plane as with Hegel; rather this "new" dialectic may be only a vain simulation of the first in accordance with Aesthetic-mindedness described in Chapter II.)

The second similarity to Freud's views lies in the fact that when "joy" occurs, the distinction between the two types of energy is dissolved and the two energies are united in a "transparent" relationship. Removal of the breach, i.e., a "synthesis," between the two energy types is, with Kierkegaard as with Freud, the ultimate source of psychic pleasure.

The basic difference is metaphysical and metapsychological. Freud saw unbound energy as seeking pleasure blindly and also as potentially self-destructive, surviving only as it is bound to the processes of the ego, whereas Kierkegaard saw the "unbound" Power of life as intentionally gracious, seeking to be bound to consciousness in a transformation yielding joy for the individual. In Kierkegaard's thought it is the dialectic of consciousness which is potentially self-destructive, not the Power which underlies it. However, these apparently clean-cut differences regarding the locus of self-destructiveness are largely confined to an a priori level of meaning; for both thinkers, the phenomenon of reality consciousness requires that the underlying Power – whatever its potential – be expressed transparently through the processes of consciousness – whatever their potential.

The Structural Model and Freedom

The final explication which is necessary to complete this discussion of Freud's view of reality as an immanent principle concerns the structural model of personality and the foregoing use of the word "valid."

An individual's internal validation of reality requires the very crucial capacity of his conscious ego to observe itself. This capacity was described in Chapter II as being a means by which one "tested the reality of things."[29] Freud's intention here is not to describe a capacity of the ego by which it becomes completely detached from all other psychic agencies, but, rather, he describes the capacity by which the conscious ego within itself can become aware of the way in which psychic energy is bound to and makes demands upon the faculties of consciousness; it also may become aware of the nature of the "endopsychic agreement" made between consciousness and those demands. By this awareness Freud also indicates that the individual who is reality-oriented gains control over the relationship – or the "endopsychic agreement" – between the faculties of consciousness and psychic energy.

Formally speaking, the separation and interaction within the ego (i.e., observer and observed, controller and controlled) that is implied by this capacity is equivalent to the relation of superego and ego-ideal to consciousness. The analysis in Chapter II indicated that these metapsychological institutions are not merely the source of guilt and conscience. In reality consciousness, they are the source of freedom. Because they are the internal representatives of external reality, they supply an Archimedean point from which one may view the demands of the primary process and the immediate environment. This internal vantage point provides the ego with the capacity to examine and control the relationships between consciousness as a response to the environment and psychic energy. When the capacity for self-observation operates "freely," testing reality, i.e., controlling the endopsychic agreement between psychic energy and conscious functions, according to pleasure sought and external demands imposed, then the individual is fully conscious. This expanded consciousness was for Freud the highest realization of man, the goal of therapy, and the criterion by which he measured all mental pathology. Correlations at this point with Kierkegaard's position were developed in Chapter III.

Summary

The foregoing discussion of Freud's views of reality consciousness has taken up the meaning of "human reality" from the three standpoints that Freud believed were required to explain any psychic phenomenon: the dynamic, the economic, and the structural. However, the discussion has maintained the restriction that each of these analytical models, as they are applied to this question, be understood from the viewpoint of the self-understanding of consciousness.

It was concluded that, dynamically, reality consciousness understood itself as " secondary process," consisting of precise functions, whose task it was to establish by means of those functions an endopsychic agreement between the influences which were imposed upon it from the " primary process " on the one hand, and from the external environment on the other.

It was concluded that, economically, the " forces of the primary processes " were the product of an independent energy resource, which in its perseity was unavailable to consciousness, but which manifested itself generally as " tension " – or more concretely as " pain " – when it was opposed; it manifested itself as " release " or " pleasure " when it was expressed. The functions of consciousness are to be understood as being in the ultimate service of this energy because their own dynamism was derived from it.

It was concluded that, structurally, the region of superego was for consciousness an " Archimedean point " by means of which it might rise above itself and observe its " dynamic " and " economic " interactions with the nonconscious influences that surrounded it. This capacity of consciousness is the nucleus of human " freedom," and is made possible because – at least from a structural point of view – there are separate " regions " in the mind to which consciousness has access.

CHAPTER

VII

THE STRUCTURAL SYNTHESIS

The foregoing chapters have taken up the question of reality consciousness as it is found in the writings of Kierkegaard and Freud. In the first place, the discussion placed special emphasis upon *human* reality in order to differentiate the reality described here from the reality of the Divine. In the second place, the discussion has placed special emphasis upon phenomena which are available to *consciousness* and thereby sought to understand human reality in terms which differentiate consciousness from its unconscious determinants. Thus these chapters have been occupied with formulating in a schematic fashion the Kierkegaardian and Freudian views of reality as confined to human experience and to the events available to consciousness.

The Definitions

The definitions of reality consciousness that were developed in the foregoing analyses are as follows:

For Kierkegaard, conscious human reality is that joyful state of existence in which one finds that the movement which underlies his thought and being so relate him to his external environment that he is capable of being independent of its categories, but at the same time capable of having, through his response to and understanding of the environment, a direct and effective interaction with it and its categories.

For Freud, a provisional definition was given in terms of an immanent psychic balance called "the reality principle." The reality principle is an endopsychic demand for agreement between the external world as it is perceived, conceptualized, judged, and/or reproduced in consciousness, and the power of the psyche, which both energizes those conscious processes and at the same time demands, through the introduction of tension that is felt as mental "pain," the eventual cooperation of those conscious processes in its own self-expression. This "demand" is felt as pain, but it is met through the agency of self-observation, which administers the relationship between conscious functions and psychic energy so that the exercise of the reality principle may maximize pleasure or satisfaction. The reality principle becomes the immanent law of one's psychic nature when the power that underlies and energizes consciousness finds satisfying and valid expression in the external world under the determination of conscious functions.

Reality Consciousness: The Boundaries

From the above definitions it is evident that there are clear-cut conceptual agreements between Kierkegaard and Freud as to the nature of reality consciousness. In the first place, neither Freud nor Kierkegaard speaks of consciousness apart from some specific content. Consciousness is always embedded within the matrix of the individual's existence; his presence in the world through the concreteness of his body is the inextricable determinant of consciousness. For Kierkegaard, it is the rescue of one's physical presence for the world and from an illusory inwardness, which is effected by the concrete finiteness of the God-man. For Freud, it is the fashion in which the psyche can most effectively preserve the demands of the body in its environment that characterizes the reality principle. Neither Freud nor Kierkegaard discusses an "essence" of consciousness; in every instance the concreteness of the place, nature, and history of one's physical presence makes consciousness what it is. Consciousness, then, is always consciousness of something; one is able to "test reality" (Freud), and "the finite is available every inch" (Kierkegaard).

Thus no statement can appropriately describe both men's thinking about the nature of reality consciousness unless it consistently maintains a contextual matrix and a content orientation as fundamental to what consciousness is.[1]

In the second place, for both men, consciousness is always "in flagranti," and it is therefore only able to be *observed* in abstraction and to the exclusion of actual temporal sequence. For Kierkegaard this is an axiomatic referent not only for the content of his thought but for the "indirect" method of communication which he used so extensively in his dialectical writings. The origin of this viewpoint for his own thinking he attributes to Trendelenburg at the outset of the *Concluding Unscientific Postscript*.[2] For Freud, it is fundamental to his "dynamic" and "economic" models that every aspect of the psyche is to be conceived as being in a constant state of activity. It was Freud's own understanding that the more static "structural" view of the psyche was only one possible model; always other models had to be employed to explain a mental phenomenon. As he wrote in *An Autobiographical Study:*

By this (metapsychology) I meant a method of approach according to which every mental process is considered in relation to three coordinates, which I described as *dynamic, topographical* [the structural model is an expanded, differentiated version of this one] and *economic* respectively: and this seemed to me to be the furthest goal that psychology could attain.[3]

Since consciousness figures into all three of these models or "coordinates," it is evident that at any particular moment its specific form is always a product of interaction, and as such is always in motion. Freud spoke specifically to this point as follows:

> Consciousness is in general in a very highly fugitive condition. What is conscious is conscious only for a moment. . . . [Persistence of an object] is explained by the fact that the stimuli of perception can persist for some time, so that in the course of it the perception of them can be repeated.[4]

> A psychical element (for instance, an idea) is not as a rule conscious for a protracted length of time. On the contrary, a state of consciousness is characteristically very transitory; an idea that is conscious now is no longer so a moment later, although it can become so again under certain conditions that are easily brought about.[5]

Thus it may be concluded that Kierkegaard and Freud are agreed on the premises that, operationally speaking, consciousness is both *focus* (subject-matter in a context) and *function* (activity or movement).

Both words, "function" and "focus," are intended to imply a momentary crystallization. "Focus" is a visual analogy based upon a particularly pleasing but momentary integration of light, distance, and spatial composition. The implication is that other things may be present in the body-environment field, but are "out of focus." Likewise "function" is also an analogy, but here the basis is biological. A function is the momentary integrated result of two or more realtively autonomous systems interacting to express or accomplish something. The implication is that other functions might be performed were the same systems interacting in a different fashion. Functioning-in-focus may describe the elementary character of consciousness at any particular instant.

This view of consciousness fits Henri Bergson's analogy of the snowflake. It is for a moment a crystal, unique and beautiful, but soon again reduced to the elements of air and water from which it was created. But Bergson's and William James's image of the "stream" of consciousness – whether moving smoothly or in saltatory fashion – is not quite appropriate. Since consciousness is an event, no streaming essence should be suggested by the above analysis. The presupposition of "movement" mentioned above means that the content which is consciousness is the creation of the body's interaction with the environment, when both "body" and "environment" are taken in the broadest sense. The reason that consciousness is not merely epiphenomenal is that it is always a creative event. It is new, an intrinsically novel synthesis of the factors which give rise to it and with respect to which it is utterly indigenous. For all its embeddedness in the matrix of experience it is incalculable, immersed in its context yet wholly serendipitous.

Reality Consciousness: The Inherent Structure

This relatively broad view of consciousness must now be differentiated in terms of its major coordinates. Thus, without subjecting the reader to the complexities of their full derivation,[6] this section will begin with a statement of the four major coordinates of functioning-in-focus that are operative in the foregoing analyses of Kierkegaard and Freud. These four coordinates will be called "modes" in order to suggest their dynamic nature, their mutual dependence, and their simultaneous distinctness.

The first will be called the " subjective mode " of consciousness in which one's expressions may be connoted by the cue word " seems." Here one may say, " It seems to me . . ." or, " I imagine . . ." or, " I need . . . ." This modality is expressed in Kierkegaard's view of reality consciousness in " feelings of joy." It is expressed in Freud's view of reality consciousness in " experience of pleasure," " experience of pain," interpreted as expressions of the primary process. Generally, immediate awareness of the power and movement which underlies consciousness presupposes the existence of this modality.

The second will be called the " empirical mode." The cue word here is " is." In this mode one presupposes shareability and " the facts of the matter." This mode figures into Kierkegaard's view first in one's ability to have a " direct and effective interaction " with the " external environment " and with its " categories." Secondly, it is the mode in which one maintains an " independence " within those categories. The first aspect permits one to make contact with what is, and the second permits one to let it be what it is without illusory sacralizations. For Freud, the empirical mode predominates in the " perception of reality " which leads to " valid expression " in the external world. " Valid expression " is possible only as one can separate validity from his wish to avoid immediate pain and maximize present pleasure. Thus, one is able to be empirical only for a temporary period during which he sees what is for what it is in itself and bargains " realistically " with it for satisfaction in the long run rather than at the moment. In general, the empirical mode presupposes concrete finitude in itself and in its distinction from the power that underlies consciousness.

The third mode may be designated " the interpretative "

in which the cue word is "means." In this mode one speaks "theoretically" or "theologically," for meaning here presupposes a systematic frame of reference and a community of persons for which "meaning" exists. For Kierkegaard, this mode appears in his emphasis upon the way in which dialectical anguish eventually gives way to "thought," "reason," and "understanding" vis-à-vis both the external environment and the "power and movement" which underlie reality consciousness. For Freud, this modality is designated by the internal conceptualization, judgment, and reproduction of the perceived environment. These three aspects of intrapsychic functioning are summed up in the phrase "self-observation" when "self" is purely reflexive, making "meaningful" relationships and reflection possible and having no reference to an internal homunculus or substantive notion of "self."

The fourth – the moral mode – is more striking than the others because of its early predominance in pathological religiousness and in the developmental history of the individual, and its apparent *disappearance* in reality consciousness. It is the "moral" mode in which the cue word is "ought." In this mode one senses or asserts a personal or social obligation. For Kierkegaard, the entire course of religious growth is motivated by a sense of "ought" with regard to one's relationship to the eternal, but in the final expression of reality consciousness there is little or no place for the modality of moral judgment. Similarly, for Freud, the religious person is driven to his beliefs and through his rituals by a sense of "ought," but the state of reality consciousness that Freud espoused completely subordinated *moral* judgment to the reality principle. For both Kierkegaard and Freud, the mode of consciousness in which one engages in the formulation of moral judgments is not among the *predominant* modes constituting reality consciousness.

What, then, is the status of the moral mode? This question can best be answered if it be first recalled that consciousness is described as functioning-in-focus and as such is a tentative crystallization or organization of psychic — or psychosocial — affairs. The three modes into and through which reality consciousness moves and which are held in balance in this state of mind are differentiated here generally in terms of their focus connoted by the cue words. It should not be forgotten that a great many things "are," "seem," and "mean" almost all at once, and that these three modes of functioning-in-focus may interrelate in a great variety of ways in a very short time. The modality of moral judgment enters the dynamics of reality consciousness as evidence that there is "a flaw" — sometimes tragic, sometimes superficial — which had not been conscious before.

Questions of "ought" do arise whether reality consciousness is a live option for an individual or not. Neither Kierkegaard nor Freud presume to say otherwise. The crucial point lies in how the "flaw" that inevitably appears affects the balance between the subjective, empirical, and interpretative modes. Under reality conditions the flaw does not demonstrate that something having been lost must now be regained. That is, the pre-flaw balance of modalities does not become a value or norm in itself, nor does it become a self-image which the imagination holds before the mind's eye. Rather, the appearance of the flaw indicates that the particular balance of modalities held previously has been lost to the past; even an accurate mnemonic reconstruction is beyond possibility. Each new restoration of reality consciousness will, so to say, bear the marks of the moral struggle through which it will have passed. It will be a novel reconstruction in and for the present.

Viewing reality consciousness as that psychic state of affairs which is repeatedly created anew through moral struggle involves a somewhat subtle understanding of the function of the moral mode in relation to reality consciousness. Fallaciously, one might have a chronic preference for "ought" as over against the other modes; or, he may feel that "ought" ought always to be considered regardless of the issue. Neither of these instances is representative of the dynamics of reality consciousness in which the vital equilibrium has been upset and is in the process of being created anew. The modality of moral judgment is compatible with the vital equilibrium of reality consciousness only when it is entered into with a sense of excitement about engaging the flaw, whether it appears from within as guilt or shame, from without in some form of social injustice, or from some combination of the two. The excitement is given a seriousness by the sense of loss of the reality state and by the actual pain involved, but it is also given the quality of positive anticipation in the expectation of the new equilibrium that will emerge.

There is some validity in noting that the sense of "ought" is usually imposed primarily upon the subjective mode, giving rise to personal obligation, or upon the empirical mode where the actualities of a given situation present social conflict. The interpretative mode generally enters in an attempt to extract the meaning from the conflict or from its resolution, though conflicts of meaning are commonplace. Preoccupation with the first mode (subjective) tends to obscure the question of what *is;* preoccupation with what *is,* on the other hand, tends to obscure what seems. Moreover, "ought" and "means" tend to be mutually exclusive as developed in Chapter III. The dynamics of consciousness will be much further elaborated in the following section. However, for him to whom reality consciousness is a live option, all four modes eventually become involved in the engagement of a flaw. A diagram of the interrelatedness between the modes as they have been discussed throughout this section is as follows:

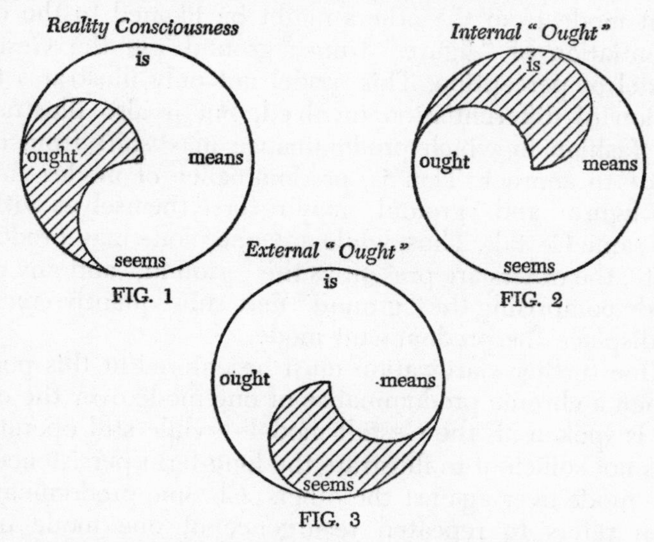

FIG. 1

FIG. 2

FIG. 3

In the diagrams the full sphere represents the full potential range of flexibility *consistent with* reality consciousness. The white area in Fig. 1 represents the predominant range of flexibility in reality consciousness itself. In Figs. 2 and 3 the white area represents the predominant range of flexibility in engagement with flaws that are either internal or external respectively. The subjective mode is predominant in the former; the empirical mode is predominant in the latter. In the instance of an internal and external flaw occurring simultaneously there would be a flexible shifting of the white area depending upon which type of flaw required the most immediate attention.

Of course, in the psychic fact of the matter these four modes are what Heinz Werner calls " syncretic "; they operate together in a unity that will not permit a perfect differentiation of one mode from all the others. The model concerns *relative* predominance of one type of functioning-in-focus over others. The differentiation of the predominant mode from the others might be likened to the differentiation of "figure" from "ground" in the Gestalt model of perception. This model not only illustrates the notion of differentiation involved, but it also illustrates the fashion in which predominance may shift from one mode to another. That is, predominance of modes shifts as "figure" and "ground" may reverse themselves within the same Gestalt. Thus, while any one mode may predominate, the others are present as the "ground," and any one mode comprising the "ground" may subsequently emerge to displace the predominant mode.

One further clarification must be entered at this point. When a chronic predominance of one mode over the others is spoken of, the Gestalt model – while still operative – is not sufficient to illustrate the long-term persistence of one mode over against the others. Chronic predominance then refers to repeated resurgence of one mode over against the others throughout a long period of time. Simple predominance in the Gestalt model refers to momentary surgence of one mode into the "figure" position; under such conditions this mode might subside as quickly as it arose.

A much fuller exposition of the model of reality consciousness will be necessary before any more definitive statement can be made. At this point, however, certain objections may have arisen which should be dealt with. In regard to Kierkegaard's position, for example, it might be assumed that Kierkegaard's notion of "existential" has here been hopelessly qualified and is now unrecognizable. Actually, if the often held stereotype of "existential" which is associated with Kierkegaard as a "melancholy Dane" and with notions of "anxiety" or "dread" were made unrecognizable, it would clarify a good deal about

Kierkegaard's intentions for the notion of " existential." There is, in fact, nothing in the stages *preceding* Religiousness B which succeeds in being truly existential as Kierkegaard asserts it must be in order to qualify as a viable alternative to essentialism in general and Hegel's " System " in particular.

The first three stages, it is true, are the propaedeutics for the final stage, and there is no possibility for getting to the final stage without them; but all of these preparatory stages are fraught with irreconcilable opposites which create painful dichotomies in human nature. However absorbing the pain may be, it never engages the individual in the fullest sense; full engagement of the individual is only possible for him in the final stage of his religious growth when he becomes the " Knight of Faith." Pain gives the illusion of total engagement, total commitment, etc., but the illusion is soon exposed for what it is, and the non-existential nature of the three preparatory stages is also exposed.

By employing the four-part typology for reality – and by renaming the " true exister " – this treatment of Kierkegaard's work has attempted to shift the contemporary emphasis away from ontological versions of existentiality (as expounded variously by Heidegger on the one hand and Sartre on the other). The fundamental position held by Kierkegaard is not really consistent with any such movements that claim to have roots in his thought. It is notable that while all these positions (and many more) claim Kierkegaard as a founding father, they go on to distinguish carefully between the adaptation they are making of Kierkegaard and their particular interest. The difference between Kierkegaard and the derivative positions often suggests that the latter writers have either failed to take Kierkegaard's work as a whole, or they have misinterpreted the problem with which he sought to deal. In fact, the systems of Heidegger and Sartre in modern philosophy are excellent examples of what Kierkegaard might have called capitulations to Aesthetic existence.

Contrary to these "systematic" treatments of Kierkegaard's seminal viewpoints, the view here developed concentrates upon the freeing of these modes of thought for the radical engagement of the world and of oneself. But, consistent with Kierkgaard's intention, such an existentiality can only be stated and developed in a functional sense at the level of the phenomenology of reality consciousness. There is no possibility for an ontological or theological systematization of Kierkegaard's viewpoint.

The second objection concerns Freud's position: it may seem that the interpretation of Freud offered here ignores his dependence upon the determinism of the dual drive theory. The answer here must be that which would be offered by any one of several so-called "ego psychologists" today. In concentrating upon the phenomenology of consciousness, this study has dwelt on certain predominant "ego functions." This is not a misconstruction or a distortion of Freud because it was his avowed goal to expand the boundaries of the ego to the place where a minimum amount of drive behavior occurred without a preliminary bargain with the ego. Thus to limit this study to ego is to concentrate upon the psychic arena in which criterional human behavior is created. Moreover, as will become evident in the following chapter, there is a creative movement toward novelty involved in the functioning of the ego. This movement not only undercuts the so-called Freudian determinism but offers the key to consciousness as functioning-in-focus.

George Santayana, in his book *Dialogues in Limbo,* has a sage in the underworld speak of a book entitled "The Wheel of Ignorance and the Lamp of Knowledge." The wheel of ignorance would have the world based on a number of principles, regarded rigidly as the spokes of a wheel; the correct view sees in these principles points of view which illuminate things first from one side and then from another like a lamp swinging in space, shedding its cover of light upon the world. Thus, he presents a metaphor for the interrelatedness of the four modes described here. He writes:

> My benefactor has entitled his profound work The Wheel of Ignorance and the Lamp of Knowledge; because, he said, the philosopher having distinguished four principles in the understanding of nature, the ignorant conceive these principles as if they were four quadrants of a wheel, on any one of which in turn the revolving edifice of nature may be supported; whereas wisdom would rather have likened those principles to four rays of a lamp suspended in the midst of the universe from the finger of Allah, and turning on its chain now to the right and now to the left; whereby its four rays, which are of diverse colors, lend to all things first one hue and then another without confusing and displacing anything.[7]

This poetical comparison may serve as an illustration of the way in which the modes of consciousness are — and are *not* — to be understood with respect to the totality of any experience.

The burden of this chapter has been a synthetic structural analysis of reality consciousness. It remains to develop the dynamic analysis in which it will be seen how the structural aspects are *interrelated*. In terms of Santayana's metaphor, we must now examine — without the finger of Allah — how the lamp turns.

SECTION THREE

Conflict and Creativity

A "RELATIONSHIP" MAY BE DEFINED AS A SITUATION THAT depends upon two or more entities, agencies, or functions, say A and B, concerning which the following three statements are true: (1) A and B would both exist even if the relationship between them were not present; (2) the relationship could not exist without A and B; and (3) the relationship itself is of a different class of phenomena from A or B.[1]

If this may be accepted as an abstract definition of relationship, the aim of this section may then be stated as follows: to formulate, from the writings of Freud and Kierkegaard, an answer to the epistemological problem: What "different class of phenomena" appears in order to integrate, or in some way bind, A (functioning of consciousness) and B (focus or subject matter)? This phenomenon cannot have been included in the processes that comprise the modalities or in the subject matter itself; yet, it must cease to exist for consciousness if either the functioning modality or the subject matter is removed.

The problem of epistemology having been stated in this fashion, the discussion now returns to an examination of the writings of Freud and Kierkegaard under the headings of the modalities of reality consciousness. It will be argued first from Kierkegaard's writings, and then from an interdisciplinary viewpoint including Freud's concepts, that the relationship designated above is an intrapsychic image. Through an internally " conceived " concrete conformation of sensory-motor and intrapsychic stimuli (the image), there is created for consciousness an internalized, essentially private, pattern of symbols, pictures, sounds, and sensations of all varieties. It is this partially " open," incommunicable image of oneself in the world that integrates one's personal past, his present environment, and his intentions into a single moment of understanding. This image constitutes consciousness from moment to moment and is in essence, therefore, the answer to the question of this chapter.

CHAPTER

VIII

The Image: CREATOR OF OBJECT AND MEANING

The Imagination and the Empirical: Kierkegaard

Empirical consciousness is characterized by the notion of " objectivity "; in this mode one acquires knowledge of objects and asserts what " is." The underlying medium and dynamic means for both the acquisition and assertion of objective knowledge is the imagination. Kierkegaard's declaration of his agreement with Fichte is his most direct expression of the dependence of objective knowledge upon the imagination:

The elder Fichte quite rightly assumed, even in relation to knowledge, that imagination is the origin of the categories.[2]

Since the covert reference here is to the Kantian categories of empirical knowledge, the indication is evident: the imagination creates the relationship between function and focus.

The translator's footnote [3] indicates, as does the subsequent context of Kierkegaard's description, that the German reference here is to the *productive Einbildungskraft* (power of the imagination). In this power, Fichte sought not only the origin of the necessary forms of thought but also the conception of an environing world, the " not-I."

Fichte's epistemological position is a consistent development from his idealistic position which worked to the conclusive disintegration of the conception of the thing-in-itself. His epistemology was that the " real series " of objects is perceived in the " ideal " series of mental representations.[4]

In declaring his agreement with this position, Kierkegaard is affirming the subjective idealism of Fichtean epistemology as the basis for all objective knowledge. Thus, the meaning of imagination in Kierkegaard's usage is specified by this declared agreement with the Fichtean view: The imagination is a broad conception which supplies the necessary forms and representations for all perception, conception, and reflection, as well as fantasy and poetic ideation. The " I," as well as the " not-I," is created for empirical consciousness by the imagination. As Fichte wrote with regard to the knowing process:

> I may then indeed say " it is thought " – and yet I can scarcely say even this; – rather, strictly speaking, I ought to say " the thought appears that I feel, perceive, think," – but by no means that I feel, perceive, think. The first only is fact; the second is an imaginary addition to the fact.[5]

In agreement with Fichte, Kierkegaard takes the imagination in the broad sense to mean any internal representation of either the focus or function of consciousness in any of its modes. Thus by the imagination one may objectify how things " seem," " mean," and " ought." This is true even when the representation of consciousness to itself is in question. The " objective " knowable " I " is as much a product of the imagination as any environmental object.

The error of Aesthetic consciousness involves not only its great predilection for the empirical modality but also its inability to discern differences among the modes and its assumption that truth is always objective. A great portion of Kierkegaard's elaborations of the Aesthetic Stage consists in illustrating how the imagination is able to represent feeling by putting it in the form of an objective representation and confusing subjective and objective modes. The first portion of *Either/Or*, especially " Don Juan," depicts the apparent indulgence in erotic feeling as really nothing more than " almost crazy wallowing in imagination." [6] The young poet in *Repetition*, whose feelings were less real than the poetic image of them, was similarly advised by Constantine. Constantine thought his failure lay in " recollecting his love." [7] Thus, by fictionalizing his feelings through the work of his imagination, the young lover was able to replace " feeling " with " thought " and to " leap over the whole of life." [8]

A more common case of how the feelings, knowledge, and will are " objectified " by imaginary representations was given in Chapter II: in regard to the sociocultural determination of religious meaning, Kierkegaard was quoted as saying that allurement into becoming one of the masses is a consequence of " the power which number exercises over the imagination." Thus to have power over the imagination is to have power over the action of the individual. The imagination represents great numbers in attendance at churches as evidence of truth; feeling, reflection, and will then capitulate, bringing the individual to act as one of the masses.

The positive use of the categories of objectivity was called by Kierkegaard " the new immediacy." Exemplification of this correct use of empirical imagination is given in Kierkegaard's description of the " Knight of Faith." Herein the " categories " are available for the Knight's knowledge of the world, and he lives in such a fashion as to make the finite fully and intensely available, " every inch." However, the Knight represents much more than this and will make a more complete appearance at the conclusion of this section.

The discussion now turns to Freud's more highly differentiated analyses of objective knowledge.

The Imagination and the Empirical: Freud

In "The Project for a Scientific Psychology," 1895, Freud wrote of knowledge of an object:

> Perception may be said to correspond to a nuclear object *plus* a motor image. While one is perceiving S (an object in the external world), one copies the movements oneself; that is to say, one innervates one's own motor image (which has been aroused to coincide with the perception) so strongly that one actually performs the movement. Thus one can speak of perception as having an "imitative value." Or the perception may arouse the memory-image of a sensation of pain of one's own, so that he feels the corresponding unpleasure and repeats the appropriate defensive movements. Here we have the "sympathetic value" of a perception.[9]

The relationship between "perception" (function, in this case) and the "nuclear object" (focus) is a "motor image."[10] It can then be seen that the image *is* the relationship[11] between functioning and its object. An image is "aroused" by the combined activity of the body's memory and stimuli from a nuclear object. The image is a different order of phenomenon from the functioning of memory or the nuclear object itself, and it would not be present as consciousness were it not for the activity of the body's memory with relation to the nuclear object.

Freud deals in a similar manner with introspective consciousness. If the sensation of pain is aroused intrapsychically, it is related to consciousness via a "memory-image" of that pain. The image includes the decisive fact that the individual feels this pain is *his own*. The intrinsic intimacy of such sensations is not lost by being imaged; rather it is precisely the " memory-image of a sensation of pain " that *is the relationship* between consciousness as a function (in this case, self-observation) and the sensations themselves. This image, be it noted, is also of a different order of phenomenon from either consciousness as function or the " economic " cause of the pain. It is " aroused " as a relationship; it is not the simple equivalent of either the so-called faculties of consciousness or of the primary process. This notion of how instincts are introduced into consciousness is present only by implication in " The Project " but is more fully developed in Freud's later papers.

From the foregoing analysis it is possible to conclude that, for Freud, as well as Kierkegaard, the image is the medium in which a relationship between any function of consciousness and its focus could be established. The image may be that which persists in consciousness – often by virtue of continual stimulation from an external object – and then is that to which conception, reflection, and judgment conform in their relationship to any given nuclear object. Consciousness in no modality conforms itself to a nuclear object in its perseity; consciousness conforms itself to an image that *is* a relationship. This means that consciousness as function may remain relatively constant while the infinite variety of total consciousness is supplied solely by its imagery.

Thus the function of consciousness responds to an image that is " aroused " or " innervated." It is this image which maintains a consistent " medium " in which to function. Consciousness traces, or " copies," as it were, the images that are aroused; and it is in tracing and differentiating the image that the " knowing " of the nuclear object takes place. The image supplies the region of which conscious functioning explores the various aspects; but judgment and reflection do not create the image, nor do they " process " it by adding to or fundamentally altering it. They simply illuminate for the awareness what is present in the image which has been " innervated." [12]

Kierkegaard stated his view that in the imagination was the origin of the categories. Freud has delineated here the fashion in which the imagery that underlies the categories begins with an " imitation " by the body of a nuclear object; perception is therefore rooted in an imaginative experience of the object; how it would be if touched, lifted, carried, and so forth. The imagined sensations of the object constitute one's consciousness of it. The Kierkegaardian analysis is consistent with the Freudian: in agreement with Fichte, Kierkegaard declares the experience of the object to be fact and the imaginary addition is knowledge *of* the object; it is a process for gaining objective knowledge very much as Freud has described here. The major difference in the viewpoints is that Kierkegaard's analysis is at a higher level of generality than Freud's.

A more complex analysis of somewhat the same type occurs in Freud's study of the perception of a person screaming.

> Let us suppose that the object presented by this perception is . . . a fellow human being [who is screaming]. . . . Cognitive or judging thought seeks for an identity with a somatic cathexis; reproductive thought seeks for an identity with a psychical cathexis (an experience of the subject's own). Judging thought operates in advance of reproductive thought, since the former furnishes the latter with ready-made facilitations to assist further associative traveling. If at the conclusion of the act of thought the indication also reaches perception, then a judgment of reality, a belief, is achieved and the aim of the whole activity is attained. [13]

Let us retrace and paraphrase the sequence described here. Initiation of the sequence that comprises consciousness is derivative from a disturbance in the perceptual field caused by a person screaming. Once the disturbance is perceived, a bodily identification is sought out as the substructure for a fully differentiated consciousness of the nature of the disturbance. This suggests the basic principle that an observer's sensory-motor imitation of the object is fundamental to a differentiated consciousness of it. Moreover, it suggests that the appropriate sensory-motor imitation is here more "objective," since it is objective bodily movements that are being imitated and since it is with one's own body – the only aspect of oneself that is simultaneously subject and object – that the imitation takes place. Obviously, since the imitation takes place in "thought," Freud is not describing an actual imitation, but an imaginative one.

The next act in the sequence – which may be interpreted as happening at the same time as the search for a "somatic cathexis" – is the search for a memory of how it seemed for the observer when he screamed at some previous time. The striking point is that apparently the imaginative somatic construction of the event is the locus of novelty in the perception; the "psychic cathexis" is merely recall. This establishment of the primacy of the somatic reflects the fundamentally neurological orientation of all Freud's earlier thinking and is essentially sound – as has been demonstrated several times during the seventy years since this passage was written.

One might describe the total act of consciousness elaborated thus far as a coalescence of an accommodation to the environment through imaginative imitation and an assimilated memory of a past experience. The coalescence "makes sense" if it allows one to adapt to the disequilibrium presented in the initial perception. The coalescence becomes "a belief" in the sense that it is a workable hypothesis about "what is going on" in the screaming person being observed.

Perhaps the most important point in this entire discussion of a conscious act is what is implied about the dynamics of consciousness itself; it is in search of "a belief." The teleology of consciousness which is implied here could be stated as a constant search for new, effective hypotheses about reality. Moreover, the teleology of consciousness is not merely adaptive in the moment but also cumulative over a long period; it seeks to strengthen its resources through the accumulations of beliefs about reality. Thus the whole of the activity is adaptive in its "outward" movement but cumulative and consequently self-differentiating in its "inward movement."

This analysis is more highly differentiated than that which Kierkegaard (or Fichte) developed, but the essential epistemological understanding is the same for both men. For Kierkegaard also imagination achieved the "belief about reality" (as opposed to purely subjective belief) because the "not-I" includes the other person as well as physical objects. Once again the general understanding is present in Kierkegaard's agreement with Fichte. Freud is more definitive about how the *productive Einbildungskraft* relates "objects" through a series of ideal representations to provide objective knowledge of a complex object such as another person.

From the latter passage quoted above it is evident that a complex nuclear object, such as another human being, can provide the occasion for arousing and innervating several types of images. These are combined in the single percept of the other individual when a "judgment of reality" is achieved. That is, one's conscious relationship to another person is made possible by a composite image.

In *Studies in Hysteria*, written at about the same time as "The Project" (1893), it is worth noting that Freud spoke of the breakdown of composite images as a source of pathology. He wrote:

What is perceived consciously [from within] is a general feeling attached to the complex; and it is this feeling that must (by a kind of " compulsion to associate ") have a connection found for it with some complex of ideas which is present in consciousness.[14]

It is evident that " general feeling " attached to an unconscious complex is what has been described earlier as an " image " of feeling which is able to be comprehended from the standpoint of consciousness as an endopsychic conformation of primary process stimuli. By stating that such an awareness, or comprehension, should be compelled to associate with " ideas " already in consciousness, Freud again indicates the presence of a teleology in relation to the power or energy that underlies consciousness; it is a striving for a belief about reality.

Though certain aspects of the " general feeling " in hysteria make it a pathological phenomenon, this discussion nevertheless puts into sharp focus the composite nature of the percept, as it was discussed in connection with " The Project." In such a composite image, feeling is bound internally to a certain object, and the composite image is posited as subsisting external to the perceiving individual; disassociating the object from its feeling may precipitate the pathological aspect of the feeling. The appropriate " association " of feeling and object is what was described above in connection with the excerpts from " The Project "; the dissolution of this association and the " *compulsion* to associate " indicate the presence of the pathology. This characteristic of hysteria is useful as an analysis of the nature of composite imagery if the pathological aspects are kept clearly in mind.

As indicated, Kierkegaard concentrated on the separation of affect from idea under the conditions of obsessional neurosis; the compulsive use of imagery and language was the outcome. Hysteria as described here represents the conversion of affect for the purpose of becoming attached to an object appropriate or otherwise; obsessionalism, through a critical use of the capacity for self-objectification, discerns the affective condition as despair and temporarily discharges it through ritualistic behavior, delusion, or doubt. The point here is that the imagination functions appropriately, according to both Kierkegaard and Freud, as uniting affect and idea; a verifiable belief about reality involves both. Imagination functions perversely in the creation of imagery that pretends to replace affect and thereby confuses the modalities obscuring any belief in reality. For instance, one may hysterically become a poet because his true erotic feelings have been separated from their appropriate bodily locus and unfortunately attached to " words." Thus Aesthetic consciousness may develop from hysterical causes due to a false objectification of affect and a consequent loss of a belief in reality.

The Image and Interpretation: Kierkegaard

The mode of interpretation in Kierkegaard is most fully elaborated in his discussion of the dialectical search for *meaning* in subjectivity. In the struggle for " true inwardness " or " subjectivity," the chief determinant is " the imagination." The imagination, according to Kierkegaard's understanding, is not a definable mental " faculty " alongside thoughts and feeling, but it is the medium through which the latter attempt to adjust the ideal and the real. Kierkegaard writes as follows:

> Speaking generally, imagination is the means by which we move in the dimension of the infinite; it is not one faculty among others; but is it, if you like, the faculty *instar omnium.*[15] Imagination reaches out to the ideal and thus provides also a medium of operation for the dialectical eros.[16]

Kierkegaard at one point indicates that the imagination provides the medium and form for the eros of reflection:

> Imagination is reflection moving in the dimension of the infinite.[17]

Hermann Diem points out that Kierkegaard gives the imagination a crucial role in achieving what has been called " the state of blessedness." Diem writes, " As a result of its connection with reflection, imagination is prevented from losing itself in the realm of boundless fantasy." [18] He then quotes Kierkegaard:

> Instead it [imagination] is turned toward the reality of individual existence which is the proper object of reflection. The power of a person's feeling, knowledge and will depends in the last resort on his imagination, on the extent to which his feeling, knowledge and will are able to reflect; hence upon imagination.[19]

Deim continues:

> Thus imagination is not only the means by which the various aspects of the ego attain the dimension of the infinite, but also the means by which they attain a correct balance. . . . Nevertheless thought is the superior element, for we must master life by the power of thinking. . . .[20] All these faculties (of the ego) are directed toward the infinite κατά δύναμιν [21] latent within them as soon as they are emancipated by the movement which eros effects therein.[22]

If imagination is the chief determinant of the dynamic of inwardness, it is evident that it is also the chief determinant of any physical action expressive of inwardness. For it is within the " true " or " subjective " self that action is conceived and directed when that action is the appropriate product of a reality consciousness. Kierkegaard writes, " The self grows out of reflection, it is self-awareness in which lies the possibility of personality." [23] The purely subjective self is only the possible self; if the ego is to " exist," action that is conceived must become real action which manifests itself externally and copes effectively. Kierkegaard writes:

> If I think that I would like to do such and such a thing, such thought is not yet act, and is eternally qualitatively distinct from an act; but it is nevertheless a possibility, in which the question of action is already reflected.[24]

He makes a further distinction regarding external activity that points up his particular fashion of thinking about how the internal and external worlds are related.

> Perhaps there is no difference between the thought and the deed from the point of view of content; but from the point of view of form this difference is essential.[25]

Thus even in manifest physical deeds the harmonizing or integrating activity of the imagination is operative. The deed is conceived by thought which is harmonized with feeling through the work of the imagination. The content of the act is perfected before the act itself takes place; so, imagination is the artificer of consciousness, enabling one to master his world effectively.

Thus, it is evident that the effective operation of the imagination is the medium and catalyst for achieving " inwardness " and a " true self "; it is also the *sine qua non* of relatedness of the " self " to the external world. It is, therefore, the medium through which " meaning " comes into being for oneself insofar as meaning consists of a relationship of oneself to the world. It is finally significant for this and the following discussion that it is the means by which the various aspects of the " ego attain a correct balance."

The Image and the Interpretative: Freud

Another important type of image with which Freud dealt in his earlier writings is the verbal image. With the introduction of language, the modality of "meaning" comes into being for Freud's thought. The verbal image was discussed first in Freud's early monograph on aphasia (1891). The portion of this work which is relevant here has been translated by James Strachey and included in the *Standard Edition.*[26] In this work Freud writes that the "word" is

> a complex presentation (*Vorstellung*), which proves to be a combination put together from auditory, visual and kinaesthetic elements. . . . A word, however, acquires its meaning by being linked to an "object-[*Ding*] presentation." . . . Philosophy tells us that an object-presentation consists in nothing more than this – that the appearance of there being a "thing" to whose various "attributes" these sense-impressions bear witness is merely due to the fact that, in enumerating the sense-impressions which we have received from an object, we also assume the possibility of their being a large number of further impressions in the same chain of associations. . . . The object-presentation is thus seen to be one which is not closed and almost one which cannot be closed, while the word-presentation is seen to be something closed, even though capable of extension. . . . The relation between word (-presentation) and object-presentation [rather than that between object and object-presentation] seems to me to deserve to be described as a "symbolic" one.[27]

Here Freud describes three phases of knowledge, or three phases of relatedness in the consciousness of an object: (1) direct relationship, which is impossible for consciousness except as sensory instruments report; (2) object presentation, which is the endopsychic organization of sensory stimuli into what has herein been called an " image "; consciousness can only posit here the distinction between (1) and (2); (3) the word, which is a closed symbol of the object-presentation.

A further Freudian insight regarding verbal imagery in the interpretative mode receives its clearest expression in his work on *The Unconscious* (1915). Concerning the interrelatedness between ideas (*Vorstellung*) and words, Freud writes:

> By being linked with words, cathexes can be provided with quality even when they represent only *relations* between presentations of objects and are thus unable to derive any quality from perceptions. Such relations, which become comprehensible only through words, form a major part of our thought-processes.[28]

Thus does Freud attribute abstract thought to the cathexis of words that in turn represent *relationships* between presentations of objects. This is especially significant, for it is here that Freud describes the fashion in which consciousness moves from perception to cognition and reflection. It is specifically by words that objects, which have no concrete perceptual relationship, are related in the mind. This " major part " of all thought processes can be restated as follows: all meaningful (to consciousness) nonperceptual relatedness between perceptual entities is presented in its perseity to the mind in the form of a verbal image. This view was foreshadowed by the interpretation made above of passages from " The Project." In *The Unconscious* it is clearly indicated that the categories which consciousness uses to delineate the aspects of any image presented to it are in fact verbal images of relationships which are not perceptible. For instance, the relationship " cause " is in its perseity imperceptible, but it does not follow that it is meaningless; it is a psychic reality which is made conscious by the presentation to consciousness of a word that denotes a type of " cause " such as dropped, pushed, forced, etc.

It is not possible to designate in Kierkegaard's writings the precise point at which empirical knowledge or knowledge which is objectifiable becomes interpretative; the description of the " word " – particularly in the first quotation – in relation to object and perceptual image indicates that Freud has made the distinction rather exactly: between the perceptual image and the word is the line between empirical and interpretative consciousness. But again, the imagination creates the word as a verbal image; so the interpretative mode is also the product of the imagination, but now, instead of creating a relationship to the external environment, it creates a means by which the environment may be transformed into symbolic communication even when the environmental object is not present. Thus does interpretation dawn, for now one becomes able to remove an object from its given context and speak of it, i.e., to give it social meaning. Moreover, it can now be placed in countless new relationships with other imagined and subsequently symbolized objects; it can be given thereby a new meaning through insight.

Kierkegaard's analysis is in essential agreement with the viewpoint that the imagination lies not only at the basis of the categories but also creates the possibility for reflection via " words." However, he is more concerned than Freud about the misuse of language and its ability to enclose the individual's mind in thought, removing him Aesthetically from his existence. Herein lies a significant agreement between Kierkegaard and Freud: language, because of its dependence upon closed symbols, is insufficient to communicate subjective knowledge fully. Hence Kierkegaard emphasizes " indirect communication " in which the beholder or listener becomes involved in his beholding and listening to the extent that he creates subjectively his own version of the event at hand, keeping it open, not locking it in an exact verbal structure. Likewise many aspects, including the final goal of therapy, depend upon the subject's creation of his *own* answer to the problems he is facing. The crucial point for the modal analysis here is the fashion in which the " word " functions to facilitate reflection beyond perception of an object; the basic concept is set forth in the first quotation regarding " words "; how it takes place is elaborated in the second.

Freud's view that abstract relationships are established by means of verbal images accounts for the manipulation of reflective notions, but the full capacity to achieve meaning requires that the internalized reality derivative from the superego – as discussed extensively above – comes into play. By means of this institution one is able to objectify his own thoughts in relationship to remembered social realities and achieve psychosocial meaning. The point to note is that the *relationships* involved are always the product of the imagination: abstract relationships from which one is able to derive a priori meaning are verbal images or symbols; social relationships are the product of composite imagery; and the internalized relationship between social reality and verbal imagery is also established by means of the imagination. But for Kierkegaard as well as Freud " imagination is prevented from losing itself in the realm of boundless fantasy " by means of reflection; by means of the capacity by which consciousness observes itself – i.e., is able to see itself in relation to social reality – the imagination is checked. In this sense, then, the imagination is self-corrective.

However, as was elaborated extensively in the discussion of pathology, the imagination is rich and facile enough to insist upon endless doubt if it cannot have boundless imagery. Reflection may check rumination and the dialectic may check an illusion, but reflection and dialectic are themselves dependent upon the imagination. Thus Kierkegaard wrote, imagination is able to achieve the infinite, for relations via images may be compounded and interrelated endlessly. The pervasiveness of imagination pushes the discussion into analysis of the " craftsmen " of consciousness, the intrinsic determinants of the imagination. Clearly, this turns our attention to an analysis of the subjective mode of consciousness.

CHAPTER

IX

The Image:
ARTIFICER OF CONSCIOUSNESS

The Imagination and the Subjective: Kierkegaard

Kierkegaard's agreement with Fichte is limited to the realm of objective knowledge. He writes in his *Journals:*

> People speak of the objective results and forget that the real philosopher is in the highest degree sub-objective. I need only name Fichte.[1]

It is to knowledge of the "sub-objective" in the highest degree to which the discussion now turns.

The "sub-objective" is by no means totally unrelated to the imagination, but it is not equivalent to a product of the imagination such as the fictional "I" of which Fichte spoke. As to this relationship between the imagination and the self (sub-objective identity of the individual), Kierkegaard writes:

> The self is reflection, and imagination is reflection, it is the counterfeit presentment of the self, which is the possibility of the self. Imagination is the possibility of all reflection, and the intensity of this medium is the possibility of the intensity of the self.[2]

Now, as Kierkegaard explains extensively in the introduction to *The Sickness Unto Death,* "the self is a relationship." The prerequisite for "relatedness" is reflection.

That is, if man is viewed under the categories of finite and infinite, and if the " finite is the limiting factor " and the " infinite is the expanding factor," then the relatedness that constitutes the self must be a relatedness between the finite and the infinite. But as such, the categories of finite and infinite are completely disjunctive; therefore, the one must be " reflected " to the other in order for there to be any relatedness. This is the role of the imagination: to present the infinite to the finite in finite terms, or to present to the finite an infinite number of finite possibilities. Thus it is that the imagination makes " the self " *possible*, but this possibility presented in the image, or in an infinite number of images, is not yet the self because the self is the relationship between the finite and the infinite, not merely the possibility of that relationship. This possibility is actualized only in the moment of " passion." Thus Kierkegaard writes:

It is only momentarily that the particular individual is able to realize existentially a unity of the infinite and the finite which transcends existence. This unity is realized in the moment of passion.[3]

In passion the existing subject is rendered infinite in the eternity of the imaginative representation, and yet he is at the same time most definitely himself.[4]

It is evident that for Kierkegaard there is a dialectic between feelings or affective conditions as well as a dialectic between concepts or imaginary representations. The disjunction is between (*a*) " passion " and (*b*) " dread " or " despair." In " passion " one is most definitely himself, but this is only " momentary." The moment there is a reflection of " passion," or of either the finite or the infinite, then the " passion " is annulled and the individual's condition becomes " despair."

Thus, despair, recognized or concealed, is the condition

of consciousness in the absence of passion. Passion, in the strictest analytical sense, can be distinguished from the imagination by means of the foregoing analysis, which posits a separation between affect and image. However, actual experience fuses them because passion strives to relieve itself through union with the image. In the fantastical "which is doubtless most closely related to fantasy, imagination," the feelings are bound to the imaginary representation, "so that a person may have a fantastic feeling."[5]

This description fits well into the discussion of hysteria developed in the foregoing chapter. Feelings have rushed to become attached to ideas in a random fashion, as Freud described. Freud's analysis was, of course, broader than this because he included in the same type of disturbance the attachment of feeling not only to such ideas but also to parts of the body, as in conversion hysteria. Here is further evidence of the functional analogy between Kierkegaard's description of the dialectics of the fantastical and Freud's description of the dynamics of hysteria. Consequently, there is more reason to assume an agreement between them on the nature of the *fusion* of affect and idea. The implication is that feeling strives to become the instructor of the imagination for the sake of obtaining a belief – however false – about reality. But the imagination has other determinants; so feeling and imagination combine in a composite image. If the condition is despair, the composite image is individual ludicrousness, conformity to the opinions of the masses (these are not an escape from the ludicrous, but merely corporate fantasies, all the more subject, therefore, to laughter), or direct expressions of despair in the senses of "suffering" and "guilt."

In the instance of the fantastic feeling, in the moment of the fantasy, the individual does not know that he is in despair. Once the fantastic feeling is reflected, or reduplicated as Kierkegaard would say, the individual may become conscious that he is in despair. Awareness of the possibility of despair is "dread."

Now consciousness of despair is decisive, so pathological religiousness as described in Chapter III is precipitated. Kierkegaard writes:

> The question whether despair is conscious or not, determines the qualitative difference between despair and despair. In its concept all despair is doubtless conscious; but from this it does not follow that he in whom it exists, he to whom it can rightly be attributed in conformity with the concept, is himself conscious of it. It is in this sense that consciousness is decisive.[6]

The concept of despair is conscious and, as such, is distinct from despair as a condition which is "unreflected." When despair is the very condition of consciousness, unreflected and therefore unapprehended by the faculties of consciousness, it imposes upon the individual with an internal immediacy so intimate that it is the prior condition of all that consciousness may subsequently become conscious of. Thus feeling, knowledge, and will are all impotent under the given condition. In the case of the despair of infinitude, they only become more fantastic and "the self" becomes more volatile.

Passion, on the other hand, takes place in a moment, in an "instant," i.e., when there is "nothing" viewed under the aspect of time.[7] When there is no distance within the individual, i.e., when there is no reflection, or when an image is so immediate as to be believed, then it may be affirmed with passion. Passion implies the *absence* of cognition and reflection; but imagination is the faculty *instar omnium:* it functions at a level deeper – at a moment *prior* – to perception and reflection.

In passion there is only the nontemporal validity of the eternal moment when "eternal" means no-time. Thus to be unified in the "eternity of the imaginative representation " is to be unified in its immediacy. Passion means no differentiation, no " distance," non-time; it is an eternal " instant." Passion is " unconscious," in that it is unreflected – once reflected in the sense of pathological religiousness, it is transformed into despair. But there are many varieties of passion. Kierkegaard's *Journal* note indicates one of the more violent varieties:

> Passion is the real thing, the real measure of man's power. And the age in which we live is wretched, because it is without passion. If, as the good Jonas Olsen [8] wrote in that memorable note, he could really hate as none had hated before, then I should consider myself fortunate in having been contemporary with him, fortunate in having become the object of that hate, – that is a real fight.[9]

The Knight of Faith, so dramatically described in *Fear and Trembling*,[10] is an example of the quiet passion of faith. As the characterization of the Knight unfolds, his feelings, thoughts, and volitions are elaborated in such a fashion as to demonstrate that he has " grasped the finite every inch " and yet retains a " solemn soul."

The summary of the argument thus far: Passion is unconscious in the sense of being unreflected. It is the basis for personal identity, just as despair is the basis for personal disparity. Thus how anything perceived or reflected takes on its personal significance, i.e., its significance for the individual himself, is dependent upon its relationship to the individual's condition, be it passion or despair. As creator of the " objective," the imagination is a potential contributor to despair; in " immediacy " it is potentially the generator of passion. However, the passion of everyday life tends to be fleeting, instantaneous, shortly giving way again to despair.

Now, in the highest form of passion – which is the " subobjective " in the " highest degree " – the passion paradoxically is made objective and therefore can endure. This is the passion of "faith." [11] Here the "object," so-called, is the paradox of the God-man which, because it is a paradox, cannot be imaginatively set at a distance from consciousness. Yet the Paradox has historical validity and social actuality, so it is not purely a rational fiction. Faith "is immediateness after reflection"; it is passion engendered by the failure of the imagination in the interpretative mode to lock the Paradox in a cognitive image.

Thus it can be said that the subjective mode of consciousness may share a composite image with objective consciousness in such a fashion as to permit the imagination to maintain the balance among the modes of consciousness. But feelings may so imperialistically dominate the total awareness of the individual that the individual becomes fantastic in either a socially acceptable fashion or in some more idiosyncratic way. "Despair" may be the underlying condition behind a fantastic idea or feeling. In such an instance, the fantastic feeling is purely objective; yet, caught *symbolically* or *imaginatively* in the fantasy is the despair that underlies it. Should consciousness then reflect upon the fantastic feeling, it would be presented with despair as a concept, that is, as a possibility. This would suffuse consciousness with "dread"—it would be dread because there would be in consciousness only possibility—only the imaginary representation of fantasy-feeling and of despair. The *dizziness* of illusory freedom or of "possibility" would then be the focus of subjective consciousness, and any differentiation would amount to a shift in modes of consciousness. By such a shift, despair, which has been posited as the determining condition of the individual, is translated into thought, feeling, and/or will. Once in despair, however, the individual cannot extricate himself; so, then, every objective image is a composite one; it is a fusion of an imaginary representation and the condition of despair.

Under the condition of despair, the individual consciousness is captive of the imagination in the objective or interpretative mode and captive of dread or despair in the subjective mode. When passion is not yet established by the Paradox, it is but a passing flash of integrity. In the moment of its suffusion through consciousness, the individual achieves an unalloyed apprehension of his own significance through subjective awareness. But in the passion of "faith," there is a replacement of despair by passion; passion becomes the underlying condition.

Thus, *functioning* in the mode of subjectivity is nothing more than direct apprehension in immediacy; one "knows" without a single marginal consideration. The *focus* is the a priori, sub-objective presentation of one's own personal significance, i.e., *identity* in passion, or *disparity* in despair, for oneself or in relationship to an object that is at least symbolically outside oneself.

Summarizing, then, Kierkegaard's understanding of the subjective mode is that the condition is, for consciousness, always *given*. Every effort of mind, will, or feeling is inevitably and irrevocably a product of the individual's condition. What is most impressive is that the imagination is the link between the condition of the individual and every thought, affect, or intention which he *expresses*. To be sure, one may become aware of his condition, but such an awareness is utterly imprisoned in subjectivity; here alone is there consciousness apart from the imagination. Since the imagination is the given for all objective or interpretative consciousness, and since the condition is the given for the subjective mode of consciousness, it is plain that consciousness even in its greatest introspective intimacy, apart from the extreme conditions of "raw feeling," is a result of at least two givens: the imagination and the condition.

However, by implication even these two are never perfectly distinct. As long as there are " appropriate " and " inappropriate " feelings, the feelings themselves have a fitness with certain ideas; apart from such ideas and attached to others, they become fantastic; so even " raw feeling " states reflect negatively the ideas or images with respect to which they are appropriate. Thus, these two psychic determinants are not really distinct, but rather two sides, as it were, of the same determination; so consciousness is shaped by the imagination and the " condition " that are determining between them, moment by moment, the delicate balance which, when reflected back from the subjective mode, ramifies into all perception, thought, and action.

The relationship between imagination and " condition " (despair or passion) is not able to be perfectly specified even with respect to *prius* and *secundus*. If one posits that the subjective mode of consciousness is necessarily more " primitive," then the priority of the condition is established. However, it should be evident by now that consciousness in the subjective mode is not necessarily " regressive "; indeed, it is in this mode that the future is created. Nevertheless, it is a dedifferentiating modality, and so does not employ the categories of the so-called " higher faculties." It can only be concluded, as has already been stated, that consciousness is what it is for the individual because of two types of a priori presentation which are made to consciousness before it is even present to itself in reflection. These presentations are the *foci of consciousness* and, as such, constitute the relationship which consciousness has to the fields of its potential subject matter. As to the field of personal subject matter, the " condition " presented in immediacy is a selective focus within the individual himself. As to the field of objective subject matter, the imagination makes the a priori presentation of a selective focus within the field of all that can be known in this manner. The *functioning* of consciousness is dedifferentiated in the first instance and very highly differentiated in the second. However, the given in both instances is the *relationship* between the knower (functioning awareness) and the known (focus).

The Image and the Subjective: Freud

It has been shown in earlier discussions of Freud's views that his understandings of perception and knowledge of either a simple or a complex object, and his analysis of interpretation through verbal forms, were given their basic form before 1900. It was shown that these conceptions are not fundamentally different from the parallel views developed by Kierkegaard almost a century earlier: indeed, they differentiate Kierkegaard's concepts and ground them in precise understandings of the role of the imagination in perception and reflection. However, it is at the decisive point of the relationship between the imagination and the "condition" that the insights achieved and articulated by Freud have their most profound relevance for the elaboration of Kierkegaard's analysis.

Some of the same lines of thought fundamental to Freud's earliest understandings of psychic images are followed up and more fully elaborated in *The Interpretation of Dreams.* In this treatment, the imagination is related to the unconscious in such a fashion as to reveal exactly the relationship between energy and imagery, the functional analogues to Kierkegaard's "condition" and imagination. Fundamental to the construction of this volume is Freud's well-known distinction between latent and manifest content in dreams. Every dream is connected through its manifest content with recent experiences, while through its latent content it is connected with more remote experiences.[12] Thus does the imagery of the dream bind the past to the present.

Dream images are, first of all, the products of " condensation." Images of persons are frequently composite unities of elements derived from the day's conscious experience. Verbal images are reified and frequently allude to an incident in connection with which the dreamed speech or verbal image was made. Thus, the dream image is a condensation not only of elements of conscious life reproduced, but also a condensation of latent meaning into manifest content.

Second, the dreamwork is described as " displacement." Freud describes this process as follows:

> A psychic force . . . strips the elements [of conscious experience] of the high psychic value of their intensity and, on the other hand, by means of over-determination, creates new significant values from elements of slight value, which new values then make their way into the dream-content.[13]

Freud concludes, " Dream-displacement and dream-condensation are the two craftsmen to whom we may chiefly ascribe the structure of the dream." [14] This all takes place at a deeper level than conscious human experience can reach. With this brief statement of Freud's concern to establish the primacy of the unconscious in the formation of dream images, the discussion must now turn to the relevance of this concern for the formation of conscious images.

The crucial connection between the unconscious and the conscious mind is based upon Freud's assertion that the conscious mind is " devoid of memory." [15] All memory images reside beneath the level of consciousness. With his strong emphasis in this volume upon the controlling powers of the unconscious, Freud contrastingly describes consciousness as a " sense organ for the perception of psychic qualities." [16] This is clearly in keeping with the Freudian view described above; consciousness functions only to trace out what is presented to it, via the image, from powers or stimuli not under its control. The unconscious controls consciousness in that memory images are regenerated unconsciously, and it is upon memory images that modal consistency depends, i.e., one imagines himself in a particular relationship with a particular object, or with a second relationship, and he is thereby able to fix his attention. That is, if modal consistency is maintained by an image, then the image must be "remembered," i.e., in the sense that it must endure. Since consciousness cannot "remember," all the modes of consciousness are dependent upon the memory image that is conjured by and repeatedly stimulated by the unconscious mind. To be sure, attention may be fixed by the repeated impingement of stimuli upon sensory receptors, but knowledge is always of an *image*, i.e., of a *relationship* to the object, not of the object per se. That is, even the image which is aroused to establish the relationship between the empirical mode of consciousness and the environmental stimuli is in this sense a product of the unconscious; a percept comes to consciousness organized and knowable, a phenomenon that, to be consistent with Freud's thinking, would be impossible without the memory image of such attributes of the percept as color, texture, and spatiotemporal determination.

The particular area of the mind in which the craftsmen of the unconscious are able to fuse the "mem-system" with external stimuli to formulate an image, indeed, to create consciousness was called by Freud "the preconscious." Thus it is through the dynamics of the preconscious system that imagery and the power or energy of the psyche are constantly engaged in the creation of consciousness. At this point "passion" is linked appropriately or inappropriately to its object, to an image of the self, to the

God-man. At this point the fine balance of feeling and idea is moment by moment created anew, or it is lost in the precipitation of emotional disturbance or of Aesthetic objectiveness. Thus, how things " seem " is of fundamental significance for the *knowledge* of what " is " and of what things " mean."

Up to this point the dynamics of consciousness have been described for the three modes which predominate in consciousness of reality, and it has been derived and stated that for Kierkegaard and Freud the imagination or the image is the chief conscious determinant in all three modes. Consciousness in the fourth mode — the moral mode in which the sense of " ought " predominates — was extensively developed in its most extreme forms in the chapters on pathological religiousness. Thus, further treatment of the subject here would be largely redundant; it will become relevant again when the creative pattern of interaction between the modes predominant in reality consciousness has been sufficiently elaborated. Then, a point for point alternative to the characteristic marks of pathological religiousness can be specified.

Kierkegaard held the view that the imagination was the means by which the aspects of the ego attained a correct balance. It is to his penetrating description of the power of the imagination to accomplish this feat and to Freud's illuminating discussions of the same phenomenon that the discussion now turns.

The Creative Image: Kierkegaard

For Kierkegaard, the resolution of pathological religiousness, as it was described in the foregoing section, centers around the imposition of the image of the God-man. For Kierkegaard, not only is the delusion of the infinite an indication of movement toward reality consciousness, but it is a necessary precondition for the reception of the God-man in "faith."

Interpretations of the "God-man" in Kierkegaard's writings are numerous;[17] but none of them brings the God-man into line with Kierkegaard's central concern, which was to understand the "how" of the proclamation, and with his basic epistemological points of view.

In order to understand the Paradox in line with these concerns, one must recall the precondition for it, namely, Religiousness A. In Religiousness A, there is a sharp disjunction made between the imaginative illusory image of the "eternal" on the one hand, and the sense of guilt – "the decisive expression" – that is imposed on the other hand. Thus, by the imagined disrelation between the self and the "external," consciousness is held tightly in the moral mode.

This decisive conflict may be stated in Kierkegaard's own dialectical fashion as that situation in which the self wants to be itself, but the infinite insists that, to be itself, it must be exactly not itself – not finite. This cannot be merely relegated to the realm of philosophy because it is an interpretative description of the problem. On the contrary, the psychology of compulsiveness and "isolation" (cf. Chapter III) properly characterizes the "sickness" of the individual in Religiousness A, and, accordingly, understanding will become his obsession. The fact that the problem of the individual's relationship to the Absolute Paradox is described as a "metaphysical crotchet" is only evidence that the interpretative mode of consciousness is predominant; transformation of the mind is understood primarily as a transformation of the *understanding*.

However, the Paradox cannot be understood. The understanding may then reject it, but such a denial is only mimicking what the Paradox has already claimed for itself. For him who is obsessed with understanding, this reflection upon the understanding's rejection of the Paradox can only lead to the conclusion that the Paradox was not understood. The individual who *must* understand will therefore return to the Paradox again and again. Each time he must reject it because it rejects the understanding; yet, the understanding cannot merely leave it, for it is obsessed with attaining the infinite. Therefore, if the Paradox is to be any more than an "acoustical illusion," it must be "bestowed."

The God-man is bestowed in a "moment,"[18] and he is bestowed as "a sign."[19] In the moment, spatiotemporal determinants are obliterated; understanding's distinctions between the finite and the infinite are led aside. In that moment, the sign of the God-man is "bestowed." He ceases to be what the understanding took him to be; he ceases to be merely a problem for obsessive thought and becomes significant for the individual himself. Kierkegaard writes:

A sign is a sign only for one who knows that it is a sign, and in the strictest sense only for one who knows what it signifies.[20]

Therefore, "the sign" points beyond itself and is not in any way what it may mean to one who simply perceives it. He who simply perceives the sign of the God-man will not recognize that it is a "sign of contradiction," and he who merely conceptualizes and reflects upon it falls into the "acoustical illusion."

Even if one does cognize the God-man as a "sign of contradiction," he has no significance for the individual himself until he is "bestowed" in the moment. This bestowal takes place as follows: in Religiousness A, the individual cannot desist from returning again and again to the Absolute Paradox. The Absolute Paradox is the "sign of contradiction," and as one gazes into Paradox:

There is something which makes it impossible for one to desist from looking — and lo! while one looks, one sees as in a mirror, one gets to see oneself, or He, the sign of contradiction, sees into the depths of one's heart while one is gazing into the contradiction. A contradiction placed directly in front of a man – if only one can get him to look upon it – is a mirror; while he is judging, what dwells within him must be revealed.[21]

But the bestowal of the God-man is " not an act of will; for all human volition has its capacity within the scope of an underlying condition." [22] Therefore, the sign of the God-man – being unable to be bestowed to the understanding because of the " acoustical illusion," and being unable to be merely perceived because it is a " sign " – is presented to consciousness as the mirror of what lies in the depths of the heart. " He reveals the thoughts of the hearts." [23] But what are the " thoughts of the heart " prior to the bestowal of the God-man? And how are they revealed?

The thoughts of the heart prior to the bestowal of the Paradox are the characteristics of Religiousness A: a sharp inward disjunction between the awareness of guilt, and the imaginative reflective awareness of the infinite and the finite. The reflective eros that sought a unity between the finite and the infinite is now threatened by the emergence of " guilt " because reflection has revealed to itself its own finitude – such is the differentiation of the conflict between the interpretative and the moral modes that predominate in the stage of Religiousness A.

But the God-man reveals the thoughts of the heart, and he reveals them as if in a mirror. That is, the dichotomy of the individual within and concerning himself is revealed to the individual, but in the mirror image the situation is completely reversed; the unsolvable conflict is resolved. The God-man is the unity between the finite and the infinite; it is a meaningful unity to the individual precisely because the internal dichotomy with which his own self-understanding was fraught was a dichotomy between the finite and the infinite. He then can believe in the God-man only as he can discern the finite and the infinite within himself; thus the sign of the God-man can be a sign only for the individual upon whom it has been bestowed, for only he knows his own "guilt," and only he knows the substance of the differentiation of that guilt; the dichotomy between the infinite and finite was between his private version of infinite and finite. The God-man relieves not only the interpretative conflict between the infinite and the finite, but he also relieves the "guilt" that controls the moral mode. In the bestowal of the Paradox, the thoughts of the hearts are revealed; but, in being revealed in reverse order, these thoughts are shown to have been in "Error." One therefore realizes that in the unity of the finite and the infinite he has not guilt but joy; the tension of Religiousness A is released in the Moment of the bestowal of the God-man.

The foregoing discussion of the bestowal of the God-man has taken up the interpretative problem prior to the moral one. However, from the idea of the Moment, it is evident that in the event of transformation both the interpretative problem and the sense of guilt are simultaneously resolved; they are simultaneously resolved in a Moment of "belief." Thus, the imagination "is the means by which the aspects of the ego attain a correct balance."

The discussion now focuses upon the role of the imagination in maintaining consciousness in a reality state. Fundamental to the Kierkegaardian definition of reality consciousness was the dictum: "Spirituality is: the power of a man's understanding over his life." [24] The relationship between "imagination" and "spirituality" can best be interpreted through the meaning of "understanding." The criterional functioning of the understanding is exemplified in Kierkegaard's writings about the Knight of Faith:

Here he is. Acquaintance made, I am introduced to him. The moment I set eyes on him I instantly push him from me, I myself leap backwards, I clasp my hands and say half aloud, "Good Lord, is this the man? . . . " He takes delight in everything, and whenever one sees him taking part in a particular pleasure, he does it with the persistence which is the mark of the earthly man whose soul is absorbed in such things. He tends to his work. So when one looks at him one might suppose that he was a clerk who had lost his soul in an intricate system of book-keeping, so precise is he. He takes a holiday on Sunday. He goes to church. No heavenly glance or any other token of the incommensurable betrays him; if one did not know him, it would be impossible to distinguish him from the rest of the congregation, for his healthy and vigorous hymn-singing proves at the most that he has a good chest. In the afternoon he walks to the forest. He takes delight in everything he sees, in the human swarm, in the new omnibuses, in the water of the Sound; when one meets him on the Beach Road one might suppose he was a shopkeeper taking his fling, that's just the way he disports himself, for he is not a poet, and I have sought in vain to detect in him the poetic incommensurability. Toward evening he walks home, his gait is as indefatigable as that of the postman. On his way he reflects that his wife has surely a special little warm dish prepared for him, e.g., a calf's head roasted, garnished with vegetables. If he were to meet a man like-minded, he could continue as far as East Gate to discourse with him about that dish, with a passion befitting a hotel chef. As it happens, he hasn't four pence to his name, and yet he fully and firmly believes that his wife has that dainty dish for him. If she had it, it would then be an invidious sight for superior people and an inspiring one for the plain man, to see him eat; for his appetite is greater than Essau's. His wife hasn't it — strangely enough, it is quite the same to him. . . . He lives as carefree as a ne'er-do-well, and yet he buys up the acceptable time at the dearest price, for he does not do the least thing except by virtue of the absurd. . . . And yet, and yet the whole earthly form he exhibits is a new creation by virtue of the absurd. He resigned everything infinitely, and then he grasped everything again by virtue of the absurd. He constantly makes the movements of infinity, but he does this with such correctness and assurance that he constantly gets the finite out of it, and there is not a second when one has a notion of anything else.[25]

The origin of the understanding is the imagination — for the imagination is the origin of the categories. Therefore, the power of the understanding is the power of the image to control the possibilities upon which the functioning of consciousness may focus. It is the power of the image to give coherent or categorical relationships to the otherwise incoherent, haphazard, and capricious influences that move through the scope of interest and attention. It is not *mere* "reason," for that would eliminate the "power . . . over his life" aspect of the above dictum; it would introduce speculation, notable "infinity," and remove concrete "finitude" from the Knight's life. It is the capacity of the imagination to organize novelty into meaningful conformations, which can then be differentiated and known, that constitutes the "power of understanding over life." This was made clear in the Knight's freedom to shift from one imaginative presentation to another, depending on his bodily states and the circumstances in which he found himself.

The foregoing indicates that the major assumption behind Kierkegaard's thinking about reality consciousness is its dependence upon the imagination. This endopsychic idealism means that every aspect of the ego is subjected to the control of whatever may perchance be conjured for the mind by the imagination. Consciousness may negate and turn away from the conjured image; but it must select another, for it cannot remain in a vacuum. The imagination provides the relationship between the understanding and the world, the self, and God. This is so because, by means of the imagination, every focus in any mode of consciousness can be finitized and "known" as an object of the empirical or interpretative modes. Therefore, movement in consciousness is objectively apprehended, but really accomplished for consciousness – before it can functionally differentiate it – by the imaginative representation.

The imaginative representation is the generator of novelty for the empirical and interpretative organization of consciousness, and it is in these modes that the individual controls his life according to the categories of the finite. So what seems to be coping with the reality of finite existence is in fact merely the differentiation of a novel, coherent image which is supplied for consciousness a priori. But there is a flexibility with respect to the imaginative representations presented; one does not get bound to an image of "Calf's head roasted, garnished with vegetables" to such an extent that its real absence precipitates despair. That is, reality consciousness moves freely from the possible to the factual and back again; the Knight "constantly makes the movements of infinity, but he does this with such correctness and assurance that he constantly gets the finite out of it."

This flexibility is not amorphous or diffuse, but it is to be understood in terms of stabilized modes of consciousness. This flexibility means an alternative mode of consciousness is always a viable option though never a necessity. Such is the case because of the ever present sense of an ultimately positive evaluation of the self. That is, the ultimate judgment of the Knight has already been made once and for all. Any movement toward "guilt" in an ultimate or chronic sense has been forfeited because the psychological limits of guilt have been reached and relieved by the God-man image. Thus, a sense of ultimate guilt has become a psychological impossibility for reality consciousness.

This situation is the basis for the sense of an ultimately positive judgment of the self as bestowed by the God-man and therefore the psychological basis of "passion," the "quiet passion of faith." Being incomprehensible to reason, this ultimately positive judgment is simply bestowed or presented to the individual as the a priori affirmation of his own consciousness in any particular aspect or mode. But, as the epistemological analysis developed thus far has shown, such an a priori affirmation is the product of the imagination; the God-man is the mirror image of the struggle of Religiousness A. In substance, i.e., in actual accumulated experience brought to bear upon the matter, each man is different, and so every man's God-man is unique for him. In form it is essentially the same in everyone: some view of the finite and some view of its negation, i.e., the infinite, are unified, and the unification frees a man of his guilt. It does not free him for euphoria, but it frees his understanding to have power over his life; it creates "spirituality" by making flexibility as well as continuity among the modes of consciousness possible.

The paradigmatic pattern for the dynamics of reality consciousness described here answers at least in part the question set down at the end of Chapter III, namely, What pattern of psychic functioning exists which characterizes nonpathological religiousness and for which sectarian language is an option? The full differentiation and basic psychological value of this paradigm emerges only through the functional analogues in Freudian thought.

The Creative Image: Freud

The power of the image to integrate diverse forces and to create a primary locus of reality, i.e., the power to "conceive" consciousness, is most succinctly disclosed in Freud's references, in *The Interpretation of Dreams,* to the writings of Herbert Silberer [26] on hypnagogic phenomena. In the studies that follow, it is possible to see with remarkable clarity the interaction and interdependence of the modal coordinates of consciousness, and, in particular, to interpret quite precisely the creative power — as well as the limits — of the imagination as the artificer of consciousness.

Freud's comments about Silberer's work are as follows:

Herbert Silberer has described a good method of directly observing the transformation of thoughts into images which occurs in dream-formation, and has thus made it possible to study in isolation this one factor of the dream-work.[27] [He] has caught the transformation of thoughts into images *in flagranti,* by forcing himself to accomplish intellectual work while in a state of fatigue and somnolence. The elaborated thought vanished, and in its place there appeared a vision which proved to be a substitute for — usually abstract — thoughts. In these experiments it so happened that the emerging image, which may be regarded as a dream-element, represented something other than the thoughts which were waiting for elaboration: namely, the exhaustion itself, the difficulty or distress involved in this work; that is, the subjective state and the manner of functioning of the person exerting himself rather than the object of his exertions. Silberer called this case, which in him occurred quite often, the "functional phenomenon," in contradistinction to the "material phenomenon" which he expected.

"For example: one afternoon I am lying, extremely sleepy, on my sofa, but I nevertheless force myself to consider a philosophical problem. I endeavour to compare the views of Kant and Schopenhauer concerning time. Owing to my somnolence I do not succeed in holding on to both trains of thought, which would have been necessary for the purposes of comparison. After several vain efforts, I once more exert all my will-power to formulate for myself the Kantian deduction in order to apply it to Schopenhauer's statement of the problem. Thereupon, I directed my attention to the latter, but when I tried to return to Kant, I found that he had again escaped me, and I tried in vain to fetch him back. And now this fruitless endeavour to rediscover the Kantian documents mislaid somewhere in my head suddenly presented itself, my eyes being closed, as in a dream-image, in the form of a visible, plastic symbol: *I demand information of a grumpy secretary, who, bent over a desk, does not allow my urgency to disturb him; half straightening himself, he gives me a look of angry refusal.*" [28]

This fundamental psychic operation is the transformation of a psychic state into a dream image. Silberer also has recorded cases in which the "material phenomenon" was reproduced. Such cases are briefly exemplified as follows:

In a state of drowsiness I contemplated an abstract topic such as the nature of transsubjectively (for all people) valid judgments. A struggle between active thinking and drowsiness sets in. The latter becomes strong enough to disrupt normal thinking and to allow – in the twilight-state so produced – the appearance of an autosymbolic phenomenon. The content of my thought presents itself to me immediately in the form of a perceptual (for an instant apparently real) picture: I see a big circle (or transparent sphere) in the air with people around it whose heads reach into the circle. This symbol expresses practically everything I was thinking of. The transsubjective value is valid for all people without exception: the circle includes all heads. The validity must have its grounds in commonality: the heads belong all in the same homogeneous sphere. Not all judgments are transsubjective: the body and limbs of the people are outside (below) the sphere as they stand on the ground as independent individuals. In the next instant I realize that it is a dream picture; the thought which gave rise to it, which I had forgotten for the moment, now comes back and I recognize the experience as an "autosymbolic" phenomenon.[29]

Other "material" examples are as follows:

Example 1. – [while in a somnolent state] I remember that I have to correct a halting passage in an essay.

Symbol. – I see myself planing a piece of wood.

Example 5. – I endeavour to call to mind the aim of certain metaphysical studies which I am proposing to undertake.

This aim, I reflect, consists in working one's way through, while seeking for the basis of existence, to ever higher forms of consciousness or levels of being.

Symbol. – I run a long knife under a cake as though to take a slice out of it.

Interpretation. – My movement with the knife signifies "working one's way through." . . . The explanation of the basis of the symbolism is as follows: At table it devolves upon me now and again to cut and distribute a cake, a business which I perform with a long, flexible knife, and which necessitates a certain amount of care. In particular, the neat extraction of the cut slices of cake presents a certain amount of difficulty; the knife must be carefully pushed *under* the slices in question (the slow "working one's way through" in order to get to the bottom). But there is yet more symbolism in the picture. The cake of the symbol was really a "dobos-cake" – that is, a cake in which the knife has to cut through several *layers* (the levels of consciousness and thought).[30]

The final illustration which will be given here concerns what Silberer called "Mixed Phenomena":

I am in a train and very tired. With my eyes closed, I am leaning against the corner of the compartment. Time and again the setting sun shines into my face. It disturbs me but I am too tired to get up and draw the shade. So I let it shine on me and watch the visual impressions that come as the sunshine hits my eyelids. Remarkably enough, the figures are different each time, but each time uniform. This is apparently a specific apperception phenomenon. I see first a mosaic of triangles, then one of squares and so on. Then I have the impression that I myself am putting together the mosaic figures in rhythmical movements. Soon I find that the rhythm is that of the axles of the train, which I hear continuously. This suggests the idea that autosymbolic pictures can be influenced by acoustic perceptions; thus a person talking to someone who is in a hypnagogic state could direct his imagery.

All of a sudden the following autosymbolic phenomenon occurs; I see an old lady, to the right, setting a table with a checkered table cloth, each square of which encloses a figure resembling one of the sun-mosaics previously mentioned; the figures are all different.

The person setting the table of my imagination with a variety of pictures represents my idea of the possibility of influencing autosymbolic phenomena from the outside.

Another symbol-source must also be mentioned here: the previous evening I had a talk with an elderly lady who told me a medley of tales of her life. It was late and I was already tired. I sat at a table with the lady on my right.[31]

This series of examples (of which there are many more in Silberer's original work) is sufficient to demonstrate the basic point which is here being made and to prepare the reader for the following discussion.

Hypnagogic imagery was first interpreted as representing the "functional" phenomenon, the entire conflictual state of mind just prior to the presentation of the hypnagogic image. It is this type of hypnagogic image which – for this discussion – will become paradigmatic for Freud's understanding of fantasy, hallucination, and delusion as attempts to construct reality consciousness. The hypnagogic image as a paradigm represents a state of conflict between idea and affect in such a fashion that paradoxically the conflict is in some sense resolved. The functional hypnagogic image binds idea and affect into a single conformation which is presented to awareness in immediacy, i.e., in such a fashion that it must be believed at least for the length of time it is able to endure. In the moment of belief the individual is relieved of the "tension" or "pain" that previously characterized his state of mind. After the image subsides, the conflict does not remain; it is, as it were, laid aside since all its elements have not been brought into a believed conciliatory relationship. Silberer notes his relief at finding that his mind found an "easier" way to accomplish the work he was trying to perform by a strenuous act of intellect and will.[32]

The creative act performed in the image's representation of the "material" phenomenon lies in the integrative fusion of diverse abstractions; the image presented in a single moment an extended train of thought. The interpretation lay in recovering the conflict present at the cognitive preimage moment and finding its resolution in the image presented. The point is that the image has now added insight by virtue of its particular organization of things and has made a solution possible where it was not possible before.

The creative power of the image to involve and transform the totality of psychic behavior is illustrated dramatically by a case history recorded by Freud. It will be noted at the conclusion of this chapter how closely the sequence developed in this case parallels the sequence in the formation of hypnagogic phenomena, and in the transformation of consciousness by the God-man.

In 1909, Freud first published "Analysis of a Phobia in a Five-year-old Boy." Here he demonstrated the effectiveness of fantasy images — the particular type of composite image which, though not always demonstrably false or impossible, yet occurs to the consciousness as a percept when there are not environmental stimuli present. In the case of Little Hans, triumphant, concluding fantasies were recorded which were manifestly impossible,[33] and in this sense the fantasies bordered on hallucinatory images. Yet the fantasies did not lock consciousness in a single, say subjective, mode of mental functioning, obliterating the cognitive and judging faculties of consciousness. Rather —

and this is the especially notable feature of these fantasies — they were able to induce a permanent reorganization of psychic functioning. Unlike dream images, from which the dreamer awakes, fantasy images were able to reorganize consciousness in a fashion from which the fantasier will not "awaken."

The explanation for this phenomenon is not, perhaps, as indubitable as the phenomenon itself, but, nevertheless, the explanation is noteworthy. Freud writes that "people's 'childhood memories' are only consolidated at a later period, usually at the age of puberty." This process is analogous in every way to the process by which a nation constructs legends about its early history. Infancy will be viewed by the individual himself in the light of the present "just as a real historian will view the past in light of the present." "This explains," says Freud, "why certain fantasies abound in seductions and assaults, where the facts will have been confined to autoerotic activities and the caresses or punishments that stimulated them." This is to say that early undifferentiated experience is given the differentiated form of object-love in the fantasy. The result is an experience of the differentiated sort which is as vivid in the individual's psychic life as if it had actually occurred in the form in which it is recalled. The theoretical aspects of this subject were of considerable concern to Freud throughout his career; enduring alterations in psychic functioning by means of the fantasy was a phenomenon that Freud repeatedly observed.[34]

The aspect of special concern to this analysis is the *phenomenon* of an effective change induced in the psyche by the fantasy. Such was exemplified in a clear-cut form by the "triumphant" fantasies of Little Hans. In these fantasies Hans's Oedipal wishes were represented as fulfilled: in the first, Hans found "a happier solution than that prescribed by destiny," and instead of putting his father out of the way granted him the same happiness he desired for himself; he made him a grandfather and married *him* to his own mother too.[35] Thus both Hans and his father could have "the mother" — their respective mothers — with no one suffering loss. In the second fantasy, Hans reversed an earlier fantasy of a plumber who had come and unscrewed the bath and stuck a borer into his stomach. In this second fantasy Hans was given a new "bigger behind" and "bigger widdler" so he could be like his daddy.[36] These fantasies represent the denouement of Hans's case and a satisfactory resolution of his conflict in relation to his father. The most remarkable point about these fantasies is the fashion in which they conclude Hans's illness. After these fantasies Hans referred to his illness only as a matter of history — "at the time when I had my nonsense."[37] Freud concludes that it was as a result of this last fantasy that the castration anxiety which lay at the root of Hans's illness was overcome.

The reconstituting work of Hans's fantasies was observed in a different form by Freud in the symptomology of paranoiac and schizophrenic patients. In his discussion of "the mechanism of paranoia," in connection with the Schreber case, Freud writes: "The delusional formation, which we take to be the pathological product, is in reality an attempt at recovery, a process of reconstruction."[38]

On this point many further references could be given,[39] but perhaps the most instructive here is that which links such attempts at reconstruction to perception and ideas. In 1917, Freud wrote as follows in "The Metapsychology of Dreams":

> The hallucinatory phase of schizophrenia has been less thoroughly studied; it seems as a rule to be of a composite nature, but in its essence it might well correspond to a fresh attempt at restitution, designed to restore a libidinal cathexis to the ideas of objects.[40]

This linkage between perception and reconstruction is based upon the restoration of a perception to accuracy in the immediacy of awareness; it is a reinnervation of a "mem-system" which presents with the force of a perception the "diversified fixation," i.e., the image that constitutes the hallucination. Because "belief in reality is bound up with perception through the senses, . . . we accept the percept of . . . [the reinnervated image] as real."[41] Thus, the hallucinatory experience — even if only in dreaming — can have a reconstituting effect as vivid and decisive as a "perceptual experience." But more than that, it may restore one's capacity to test reality.

Summary: The Hypnagogic Paradigm

In this section, consciousness has been discussed primarily in its dependence upon the creative capacities of hypnagogic, hallucinatory, delusional, and fantasy images. The first consideration was that the immediacy with which these phenomena imposed themselves upon consciousness involved a dedifferentiation and reconstruction of reflective or abstract notions in conflict, either with themselves or with a feeling state. Yet decisive cognitive elements in the conflict were retained: the visual imagery, verbal and ideational forms, and categories of knowledge such as cause and effect.

The origin of the images is the body-environment matrix; the world of the senses together with kinesthetic sensations and motor activity provide the quantitative and qualitative substance of the image. This great mass of sensations is organized by the body's activity in the world in that it is the body from which all notions of space and duration are derived. "Internally" the body creates all its sensations by the power or energy that motivates it. The creation of an organized sensory perception and a coherent pattern of reflection and interpretation are fundamentally the body's relationship to the world translated into the imagination.

Thus, the imagination originates from within the body, but its *telos* is to return to the body in action. Consciousness strives for a " belief about reality "; it strives at least to " reflect action as a possibility," if not to act in deed. Thus, the imagination is the crux, the very quick of consciousness where in a moment the vast world of sensations that impinge upon the mind are re-created in representative objects and translated into action upon the body-environment matrix from which they originated.

In the course of moving from the body-environment matrix into action, the imaginings of consciousness are structured by memory images and by " known " patterns of bodily interaction with the environment. (The actual derivations of structure are most adequately described developmentally in the works of Jean Piaget, especially *Play, Dreams and Imitations in Childhood* [W. W. Norton & Company, Inc., 1962], and described phenomenologically in the works of Maurice Merleau-Ponty, *The Structure of Behavior* [Beacon Press, Inc., 1963] and *Phenomenology of Perception* [London: Routledge & Kegan Paul, Ltd., 1962].) Reflection is structured by language and by internalized images of social actuality and tangible things.

It is through the imagination that psychic power is translated into psychic structure and structure is made available for the purposes of psychic power. Elaborations of the structure or subtle redirections of the intentions of power are in the final analysis dependent upon the ability of the imagination to create an image, a belief about reality, that can be translated into action.

Since the range of investigation here has been confined to consciousness, these types of imagery must be interpreted in a fashion similar to that employed by Silberer in analyzing hypnagogic imagery, i.e., from the standpoint of their interrelatedness with empirical and interpretative consciousness. This is not an arbitrary line of analysis; the interpretation of hypnagogic, fantasy, hallucinatory, and some delusional images by Silberer's method was not only theoretically affirmed by Freud, but also was a method he himself employed.[42] This method of interpretation as it is used here simply attempts to restore for reflection and judgment the basic conflict which gave rise to the image, and to discern how the conflict-as-resolved has been represented symbolically in the particular image under question. It is especially significant here because it is the interpretation of imagery that is, as will be seen, indigenous to the pattern of reality consciousness itself. Since the interpretation of hypnagogic imagery cited above has expounded and applied this method, and since this seems to be the simplest and most precise development of the sequence through which consciousness passes in its discovery and perusal of reality, the following steps, taken in sequence, will be referred to as the hypnagogic paradigm.

1. The paradigm is initiated with conscious conflict. This initial conflict may be in any mode – for instance, a conflict in the interpretation of transsubjective values, or a conflict between modes as the subjective wish to sleep versus interpretations of " time," or a conflict involving all three modes (objective, interpretative, and subjective) as in the " mixed phenomena " illustration.

The conflict in the case of Little Hans involved all four modes with the precipitating conflict appearing between the moral mode (Hans's mother threatened him with castration if he continued to touch his " widdler ") and the subjective mode, in which he " wishes " to be like his father. Hans's " nonsense," i.e., his phobic symptoms, persists until an *interpretation*, stating his basic conflict, is made to him by his father (under Freud's instruction).

When the subjective wish is translated into an interpretation and set in contrast to what actually was the case, i.e., the empirical was set in conflict with its opposite (the subjective), then the conflict becomes conscious, fitting the initial step of the paradigm.

The conflict in the Kierkegaardian paradigm has been developed extensively in conjunction with the " Stages." Clearly, the conflict, when it reaches Religiousness A, again involves all modes. The *empirical* fact of the God-man is insisted upon even if it be only a *nota bene* washed up on the shore in a bottle, asserting, " We have believed that in such and such a year God appeared among us in the humble figure of a servant, that he lived and taught in our community and finally died." This fact, empirically known, is set in conflict with the *subjective* condition of despair expressed first in " suffering " and then in " guilt "; the subjective condition is dialectically translated into images of the eternal and the infinite. The *moral* mode enters the conflict in the Ethical Stage and reaches its greatest intensity and predominance in Religiousness A, and the *interpretative* mode tries " desperately " to reason the Paradox into coherent meaning and out of existence, i.e., out of subjective significance and out of empirical possibility. These conflicts are precisely in the process of expanding consciousness; so here, too, the first condition of the hypnagogic paradigm is met.

The basic principle is that consciousness achieves a resolution of those conflicts which are made known to it consciously, but when there is a transparent relationship between the conflict which is " made known " and the conflict which is unconscious – or locked in preconsciousness – then the totality of psychic behavior is decisively affected.

2. Following a pause, the second step in the sequence is the emergence of the image that accomplishes the work

left unfinished in the conflict; it puts into a single symbolic conformation (the image), presented perhaps in a single moment of time, the solution to the predominant conflict before consciousness. But the image adds nothing which was not present in consciousness prior to the conflict; the feeling state, memories – or "mem-systems" to use Freud's phrase – combine with cognitive and perceptual images to present an intrinsically novel composition of symbols, derivative from all modes but from nowhere other than the modes. In the craftsmanship of the symbolic composition, i.e., in the arrangement, lies the novelty, i.e., the solution; the substance is inevitably familiar. Such is the case with all examples from Silberer's studies presented above.

The fantasies of Little Hans appeared with a symbolism rich enough to resolve the fundamental conflict: the subjective wish to supplant his father versus the radical empirical differences between father and son. The fantasies that resolved the conflict did not come into being until the conflict itself had been very plain to Little Hans himself; he wanted to be married to his mommy, but his mommy had threatened castration; he wanted to have children and to be like his daddy, but his daddy was too "big" for him to replace. Once the conflict had been made fully conscious for him through the interpretation, the hypnagogic paradigm could come into play. The difference is merely that the image is a fantasy – not conceived in drowsiness – but merely in reverie. The symbolic resolution in the fantasies is taken from nowhere other than the conflict as it was finally made fully conscious for Hans prior to the first fantasy.

For the paradigm which Kierkegaard presents, the image is that of the God-man whose prerequisites are that the one upon whom he is bestowed first pass through the other stages along life's way. That is, the ultimate in despair must be made fully conscious in order that the *mirror image* (i.e., nothing new is present; the old is merely rearranged) which emerges not resolve an irrelevant or trivial conflict which consciousness may momentarily be facing; one must know the finite and the infinite in their respective extremes; otherwise the image will not have solved a great enough problem to exhaust the totality of one's existence and to supply the *ultimate* positive judgment.

Thus the principle here in the Kierkegaardian paradigm is the same as that of the hypnagogic and the case of Hans: the images which appear *de novo,* having no explicable connection for the subject himself with the conscious state that preceded them (Hans's phobias, for instance) are not successfully creative but disruptive for reality consciousness. Therefore, it is suggested that one may induce a creative response by bringing to consciousness an appropriate conflict; moreover, one may correct a "fantastic" image by indicating that its roots, being unconscious to the beholder, need to be discovered before the real insight concealed in the fantasy can be grasped in a valid creative image.

3. In the hypnagogic paradigm there is a release of tension, occurring simultaneously with the appearance of the image; the conflict is resolved and the tension that is the by-product of the conflict disappears.

The anxiety induced by the mother's threat of castration is the specific tension that is resolved when Little Hans succeeds in "marrying" her and gaining a full identification with his father through the fantasy. In the first fantasy he supplants the father, but subtly succeeds in reducing the father to his own level of Oedipal motivation and to an identification with himself. In the second, he is fully identified with the father in terms of manly "equipment" and, more than that, he has nothing to fear from castration because now he is too big to worry and "happily married." Failure of the image to release tension is disruptive of reality consciousness (as again in the case of Hans's phobic fantasies), increasing tension and compounding the conflict.

For the Kierkegaardian paradigm as well, the release of tension is a marked characteristic of the bestowal of the God-man. Kierkegaard says explicitly that the greatest tension possible is to be developed up to the point at which the Paradox appears. Then the release may be one of "joy."

The principle is that if the release fails to appear, then it is evident that the conscious conflict was not the one resolved by the emergent image; an unconscious influence (a conflict concealed from the subject) has entered disruptively into the pattern of reality consciousness. As mentioned, Hans's phobias are exemplary of this type of flaw in paradigmatic consciousness.

4. The upshot of release is the restoration of the vital balance among the predominant modes in reality consciousness. In the hypnagogic paradigm, consciousness "awakens" to the recognition that the conflict has been resolved in the image and enlivened to the empirical world. Since the conflict, hitherto so absorbing in drawing consciousness away from the empirical modality, has now been solved through the creative power of the image, new aspects of reality – and new conflicts – can be explored and readily engaged.

In the case of Little Hans, the striking situation is that the fantasies restored reality to the child, making it possible for him to completely lay aside his "nonsense"; he was restored to his senses.

In the instance of Kierkegaard's paradigm, the pathological religiousness represented in all three previous stages is completely and radically obliterated by the Paradox, and the finite becomes available " every inch "; one's understanding gains power over his life.

Clearly, if one comes this far and fails to gain the finite, he would be locked in a single image; he would become obsessed, let us say, with the God-man, qua image, rather than restored to finite existence by its bestowal. Of course, one could not moralistically assert the finite as a " good " thing; it must be the " given," a product of the image; otherwise, in itself, it becomes an obsession.

5. Finally, the hypnagogic paradigm asserts the significance of interpretation. Without interpretation the relationship between the conflict, the image, the release, and the restoration of the empirical are left entirely to chance. Fundamentally, it is by means of interpretation that the creative image moves beyond immediacy into verbal symbols and into community. Thus Silberer's own interpretations not only make his experiences public; but for him alone, putting the symbols into verbal forms closes the image and completes the sequence which would otherwise have been left open; the meaning would have been left in the image and, therefore, diffuse.

In the case of Little Hans, it was as the fantasies were interpreted to the boy by his father that they were closed. Once the accurate meaning became public, then the conflict-resolving image was fixed in language, and thereby was the resolution also more permanently established.

In Kierkegaard's paradigm, to appropriate the God-man without an understanding of what had happened in its bestowal would be to fall into error regarding the revelation and reveal perhaps that it was no revelation at all. This is precisely Kierkegaard's criticism of Magister Adler who supposedly received a direct revelation from God; he was " led astray by his *conception* of what it is to be a theological candidate." Kierkegaard, in this same connection, writes:

Emotion which is Christian is checked by the definition of concepts, and when emotion is transposed or expressed in words in order to be communicated, this transposition must occur constantly with the definition of the concepts.[43]

The principle implied is that a misinterpretation of a revelation – or of any creative image which enlivens the empirical world according to the four preceding steps – may be disruptive to reality consciousness if it fails to keep the " meaning " of the image entirely indigenous to the context of the conflict in which it emerged.

It should now be evident that these five steps of the hypnagogic paradigm describe in sequence a fundamental pattern of reality consciousness which combines both the structural and the dynamic aspects. This paradigm catches in " slow motion " a general pattern of reality consciousness, whether it be functioning at such tremendously great speed that the image is hardly noticed or it be functioning at a relatively slow and disturbed rate, as in pathological religiousness, that only over the period of several years gradually restores – one fragmentary image at a time – the full predominance of the empirical, interpretative, and subjective modes.

The *moral* mode may precede the others in the sense that there is by definition in this mode a conflict present; but whatever the conflict, the *subjective* must act first, creating the image that will allow one to move effectively into the *empirical* as a given and thence to the meaning or *interpretation* of the thought adduced. Since the empirical must be a given and since meaning must always be indigenous to the imaginative resolution of the conflict, it is evident that reality consciousness is fundamentally the imagination; or more dynamically, it is the fusion of conflict and creativity moving toward a belief in reality. Clearly, meaning becomes a matter of " ought " when the internalized reality (conscience) does not suit what is or what seems to be the case. And the circle is simultaneously completed and begun again as the moral conflict is precipitated. Nevertheless, reality consciousness – however frequently disturbed – may be viewed both from the Freudian and the Kierkegaardian standpoints as ceaselessly emerging, striving to establish the predominance of the three modes, subjective, empirical, and interpretative, interrelated according to the hypnagogic paradigm. Thus does conflict eventuate in realistic action through the creative power of the imagination.

SECTION FOUR

Conclusions

In order to put reality consciousness into its appropriate context, the discussion must conclude by applying and clarifying it, at least briefly, in circumstances where both its critical and constructive contributions may come to light. Succinctly, this section speaks to the question, So what? The answer will be put in terms of the significance of the paradigm when it is brought into relationship with intrinsically related concepts, issues in theology and ethics, problems in other interdisciplinary studies, and the educational dimension of Christian thought.

CHAPTER

X

RAMIFICATIONS OF THE PARADIGM: I

Two words that appear at crucial points in common parlance, as well as in theological and ethical discourse, are illuminated by an application of the foregoing analysis of reality consciousness. These are " conscience " and " freedom "; clarification of the phenomena designated by these words is developed in the following two sections.

Conscience and Meaning

Freud declared:

The super-ego continues to act the rôle of an external world toward the ego, although it has become part of the internal world.[1]

What is described here is the structural institution of the psyche which provides the foundation for the functions of self-observation, reflection, and the interpretation of meaning; the latter two functions are rooted in the first, the " formal " aspect of the superego (see Waelder's statements in Chapter III), self-observation. Moreover, for Freudian thought, the superego and its derivatives are, through the formal aspect of self-observation, the source of conscience. For consciousness, then, the superego is the source of two distinct modes: the interpretation of meaning and the formation of moral judgment; and the capacity for *self-observation* is the means by which superego becomes a determinant in both modes of consciousness. It must now be seen how imagery as the artificer of consciousness in all its modes underlies and in effect creates the image of self-observation, thereby relating the superego to an act of consciousness. By studying Freud's writings on " conscience " in relation to superego, the role of the image as the producer of both meaning and of conscience will emerge.

Freud wrote as follows:

It would not surprise us if we were to find a special psychical agency which performs the task of seeing that narcissistic satisfaction from the ego ideal is ensured and which, with this end in view, constantly watches the actual ego and measures it by that ideal. If such an agency does exist, we cannot possibly come upon it as a *discovery* – we can only *recognize* it; for we may reflect that what we call our " conscience " has the required characteristics. Recognition of this agency enables us to understand the so-called " delusions of being noticed " or more correctly, of being *watched,* which are such striking symptoms in the paranoid diseases and which may also occur as an isolated form of illness, or intercalated in a transference neurosis. . . . A power of this kind, watching, discovering and criticizing all our intentions, does really exist. Indeed, it exists in every one of us in normal life. . . .

The complaints made by paranoics also show that at bottom the self-criticism of conscience coincides with the self-observation on which it is based. Thus the activity of the mind which has taken over the function of conscience has also placed itself at the service of internal research, which furnishes philosophy with the material for its intellectual operations. . . .

It will certainly be of importance to us if evidence of the activity of this critically observing agency – which becomes heightened into conscience and philosophic introspection –

can be found in other fields as well. I will mention here what Herbert Silberer has called the "functional phenomenon," one of the few indisputably valuable additions to the theory of dreams. Silberer, as we know, has shown that in states between sleeping and waking we can directly observe the translation of thoughts into visual images, but that in these circumstances we frequently have a representation, not of a thought-content, but of the actual state (willingness, fatigue, etc.) of the person who is struggling against sleep. Similarly, he has shown that the conclusions of some dreams or some divisions in their content merely signify the dreamer's own perception of his sleeping and waking. Silberer has thus demonstrated the part played by observation – in the sense of the paranoic's delusions of being watched – in the formation of dreams.[2]

In a later paper entitled "A Child Is Being Beaten" (1917), Freud wrote as follows about the agency that he later designated "super-ego":

According to our present orientation in the structure of the ego, which is as yet uncertain, we should assign it (the sense of guilt) to the agency in the mind which sets itself up as a critical conscience over against the rest of the ego, which produces Silberer's functional phenomenon in dreams, and which cuts itself off in delusions of being watched.[3]

As indicated, conscience or introspective consciousness is superego and ego ideal for the structural analysis of the psyche. However, the formal aspect of the superego, self-observation, is dynamically speaking, a "division" which can be represented graphically through visual imagery in dreams or in hypnagogic phenomena. Such a division was grasped by Silberer in his interpretation of "the old woman" in the earlier illustration designated "mixed phenomena." The woman pictures external influence and the reflection upon possible manipulation of imagery, but in a single presentation both Silberer's consciousness of the sunshine mosaic and the reflection upon external influence are combined and presented at once as consciousness. Thus the " division " is retained imaginatively, but the image is presented " all at once."

The primary point is that reflection, even " self-observation," is not a particular spatiotemporal posture which is taken inside the head; consciousness cannot, as some mechanical models imply, slip off somewhere to another corner of the head and watch itself work. Self-observation is primarily an image – a mixed phenomenon, usually more complex than Silberer's illustration – in which one's consciousness of any previous moment is combined symbolically with an evaluative or objective " institution " – the superego or its equivalents – which is also present in the image symbolically. The combination is " presented " (*vorstellen*) as a single conformation which is " believed " as a hypothesis about reality.

Such a " judgment " by one's internalized environment, issued from its residence in the unconscious, is the sole means by which one may see himself reflected. Yet the " judgment " is presented as an image at the level of the preconscious; and the image contains symbolically within its figures the condemnation or praise of " conscience " – the positive or negative evaluation of an idea or thought about the present environment, about one's own body, or about any number of self-understandings.

Then, once the image is presented, it may, by association, be put in " words " which, as stated, acquire their meaning by being linked to objects. (Originally they were attached to perceptual images, not to reflective images.) The word is particularly well-suited to its task, since it is a " complex presentation," " a combination put together from auditory, visual, and kinaesthetic elements." Moreover, the word is able to designate nonobjective aspects of the image such as the abstract relations between objects. When the image has been reduced to words, it is "closed," "objectified," and shareable; under paradigmatic circumstances it has "*meaning*."

Thus, even a complex philosophical system, for instance, is created by "closing" the imaginative conformations — the symbolic judgments about reality — from which it was translated, into verbal forms. Because Hegel failed to recognize this, he failed to note the dependence of his System not only upon his imagination but also upon the total body-environment matrix in which he existed. This, Hegel's fundamental error, Kierkegaard spent a lifetime exposing.

Essentially the same grounds that have been adduced from Freud's thought above were the basis of Kierkegaard's position. The major difference was that he, unlike Freud, never conceived of a topographical model of the psyche, nor did he develop "meaning" in terms of the unconscious appropriation of parental figures and social reality. But these differences appear at the metapsychological level and have to do with ontogenetic development; they do not alter the essential agreement between Kierkegaard and Freud on the phenomenology of consciousness and the imaginative foundations of meaning. Eventually, for both Kierkegaard and Freud, the act of discovering "meaning" — of making an interpretation — is completed when the "belief," which is created by the image, is confirmed in the body's encounter with the environment through some type of action, verbal or motor, suppressed or manifest.

Such meaningful relatedness is transformed into a matter of *conscience* in two ways:

1. If the image in which one's self is reflected cannot be closed into language, i.e., cannot in its major components become meaningful for another, then the power of self-observation has failed, and the individual must conclude that he is being "watched" or seen in a way that he him-

self cannot understand. When this failure to attain meaning is reflected in a second act of self-observation, then the *discontinuity* between the failure of the first belief about reality and the preestablished internalized sense of reality – or one's idea of himself – produces "conscience" as a sense of shame or embarrassment. If the condition underlying consciousness is "despair" (Kierkegaard) or anxiety (Freud), then the discontinuity will produce, as a matter of course, a "bad" conscience; under conditions of "faith" one engages the conflict according to the paradigm.

2. "Guilt" is a more intense matter. For Kierkegaard, the condition of despair made all efforts to achieve full, i.e., existential, "meaning" impossible. One might observe himself endlessly, altering his beliefs about reality appropriately for every new insight, but never achieve a "transparent" relationship between his imagined self and the existence in which he found himself. The origins of this condition are God's relationship to Adam; so one is guilty not so much because of a failure in any *particular* attempt to attain "meaning," but, rather, the nature of one's condition (despair) is that of "guilt" in relationship to its origins on the one hand, and in relationship to every attempt at "meaning" on the other.

Freud's analysis is in fundamental agreement with this view of guilt at the phenomenological level; however, by his reductionistic metapsychological analyses he has asserted that God's relationship to Adam is a disguised relationship of every man to his father. Thus the origins of guilt are not cosmological or world-historical, but psychological and developmental. The reductionism of this position must be excluded from the discussion as unfounded (see Chapters I and III); however, the observation, apart from its reductionistic intent, is analogous to Kierkegaard's view that every man re-creates Adam's experience in his own. Adam's was different primarily in that his – being first – was not influenced by the communities and institutions of men whose guilt had already forced them to adopt some corporate pathology. Most significant, both Freud and Kierkegaard turned to an analysis of origins – unconscious or supernatural – to explain the state of guilt; evidently both observed that its roots are deeper than memory.

Self-observation shifts from meaning and becomes a matter of conscience (*a*) when it is externally falsified by another or by a community and (*b*) when it is an observation of the *condition* of consciousness, i.e., its underlying despair that persists even when "meanings" *are* achieved. The first is an occasion, the second is a state; their interrelation may be described by asserting that the state of guilt produces shame on occasion.

Thus a sense of conscience is fundamentally a sense of the loss of meaningful relatedness. Guilt may be given meaning; meaning may precipitate guilt; but the two modes cannot coexist, for, to the extent that there is meaningful relatedness, there is no consciousness of guilt. In Freud's view, the aggravation of a guilt-producing conscience may become unbearable. Then the internal "eyes" will be projected and become the eyes of persons in the environment; they, rather than conscience, will watch the self. By this act one's isolation in paranoid delusional thought is initiated. These consequences of guilt are essentially what Kierkegaard described: guilt, as the decisive expression of despair, creates a radical social isolation, and the rationalization for the isolation is essentially delusional because of its false interpretation of the "eternal." However, the point made earlier was that when the imagination succeeds in restoring meaningful relatedness, consciousness, through the combination of conflict and creativity, has been expanded; and to that extent it has also expanded the boundaries of meaning. Thus conscience, while it conflicts with meaning, acts, may we say, like an intense heat, " firing " consciousness and permitting it to be either distorted or hammered into the shape of reality.

The Paradigm as Freedom

It was stated earlier (Chapter III) that freedom stands in a dialectical relationship to guilt. However, the freedom spoken of at that point was deemed illusory, i.e., not productive of a belief about reality, but rendering only dizziness, which is at best an abortive freedom. Thus freedom must now be reinterpreted in the light of the analysis of the hypnagogic paradigm for reality consciousness.

It has been stated that consciousness is primarily imagination, but in reality it is imaginative, not illusory. It is a creative act in which disparate conflictual elements of experience are integrated in a single moment; in that moment, conflict is resolved and tension is released, for the mind has bestowed upon it a belief about reality. This belief is " the known," reflected upon by being reconstructed and fitted into a relationship with the internalized structures of the external world. The result is a " judgment " about " the known," that is substantively a second image incorporating the first. This latter image is translated by association into words, action, or resistance to either, and it is then tested against the body-environment matrix in which it was created. Thus does one create, and step into, his version of his place in the world.

In this context, freedom can be developed somewhat beyond Waelder's statements in Chapter III. In the creative act of image formation lies the locus of freedom. No new element is introduced in the image which has not been extracted from the individual's experience, but in an imaginative symbolic reorganization of the familiar – an achievement by the same "craftsmen" who created the dream, but here at a preconscious level – the image sets the dimensions of the environment into unique patterns of relatedness and simultaneously alters the way in which the body-environment matrix is known. The presence of novelty is simultaneously the presence of freedom.

The particular aspect of freedom of which Waelder spoke is the test of the novel image by the incorporated external world; this is an important aspect of freedom, i.e., freedom from distortions of need and desire. But Waelder's alternative seems to be subjection to a determinism by the internalized environment, the substitution of one kind of determinism for another. The epistemological analysis of this volume has suggested that freedom within environmental structures – both internal and external – and from desire or need simultaneously is the gift of the image that synthesizes both in a belief about reality. The belief is novel, uniquely one's own, because of the individual's unique place in the world and his unique personal history; yet it is true to the matrix of experience because a "judgment" by the internalized portion of the external environment is integrated into the image that constitutes the belief according to its *telos*. While words or actions make the test of reality, they "close" the image to do so, and in effect subject the uniqueness and novelty that was secured by the image to the conformity demanded by everyday speech. Thus, the imagery that constitutes consciousness repeatedly restructures and integrates, at incredible speeds, the body's place in the environment, and therein, quite apart from apparent conformity or nonconformity, lies one's freedom.

Silberer's studies caught the process of thought "*in flagranti*" and enabled the sequence to be studied. Consequently, it may be said that intentional speech or action represents the conclusion of a thought; the pause that precedes such behavior is a very low-keyed hypnagogic moment in which the imagery-creating consciousness is reconstructed in the face of internal conflict or external challenge.

Every conscious human being is in some measure free in that he imagines. But a measure of freedom is the hypnagogic paradigm, i.e., To what extent does consciousness move through the five steps of the paradigm without distortion or violation of the five principles? Especially, does the integration achieved by the image in a reflected belief about reality release tension and restore flexible utilization of the modes of consciousness for coping with the empirical world in action? Is meaningful relatedness the outcome? In effect, does the image work in such a fashion as to permit the paradigm to be repeated in full over and over again? One is free indeed when no mode of consciousness can present a challenge or conflict that cannot be faced paradigmatically; one can then, in Kierkegaard's phrase, " think every thought whole."

The primary locus of freedom is the integrative power of the imagination, but this freedom can be distorted at any phase of the paradigmatic pattern of thought. That is, due to despair, the image may be twisted into the creation of illusory visions which inspire conviction only in symbolized, nonempirical realities and force " meaning " into delusional defenses against guilt. Only if the condition at the base of the psyche is the quiet " passion of faith " — or its functional equivalent — is freedom fully alive. No conflict, no challenge, no conformity, can disturb reality consciousness by forcing it into strict bondage to need, to internal environment, or, indeed, even to the immediate external environment. Freedom, in the final analysis, then, consists in one's ability to so perform the paradigm that in the face of unanticipated challenge or conflict he will be able to perform it anew; thus, paradigmatic freedom is self-authenticating.

In this way does the paradigm – in sharp contrast to pathological religiousness – make possible meaningful relatedness with another. In Kierkegaard's terms, reality consciousness is "transparent," making the imaginative integration of oneself available to self-observation and potentially to communication. Thus is one capable in paradigmatic freedom of being free for community, or free to avoid or correct it if it represents merely "parallel play," or "collective monologue."

Image and "Blik"

It is particularly relevant to this analysis that Paul van Buren (*The Secular Meaning of the Gospel* [The Macmillan Company, 1963]) should develop a view of "freedom" based upon an epistemology of the "blik." In brief, the "blik" is a preverbal orientation or commitment to see the world in a certain way. As it was invented by R. M. Hare, and as it is used by van Buren, there is no distinction between a sane and an insane "blik" because, of course, basic orientations are not verifiable. When "in a situation of discernment" one gets a "blik" focus upon the history of Jesus and sees "Jesus in a *new* way," sharing in the freedom that had been his, then one also becomes free as Jesus was free, i.e., free to be for others.

In the light of the hypnagogic paradigm, van Buren's view of freedom commends itself at the point of the "blik," i.e., the locus of freedom is at the correct level of psychic life. However, it flounders on its failure to discern a difference between a sane and an insane "blik." In other words, this analysis fails to make the distinctions that Freud and Kierkegaard so carefully made between illusory freedom and real freedom. This is due to the fact that the propaedeutics of the " blik " are not developed, nor are the consequences spelled out.

As to propaedeutics, van Buren's analysis would imply that one might wake up one day and suddenly – " blik "! The freedom of the historical Jesus has been " caught " because it is " contagious." Apart from the object to which it is directed, it is not essentially different from a " blik " that says, " Blondes are more fun," and brings one to a commitment to marry a blonde in order that he may have fun as the blonde does – assuming that fun can also be contagious.

Rather, from the viewpoint of the paradigm, the Christian " blik " will inevitably be the product of a body-environment conflict of which the individual was *conscious* prior to the " blik " and for which the " blik " is the essentially creative and thoroughly indigenous resolution. If this be the case, it is vitally important to point out, as van Buren does not, that the particular struggles of, let us say, Peter with Jesus – as both living and dead – prior to Easter are as decisive for his Easter " blik " as the fact of the " blik " itself; the " blik " solves only Peter's particular conscious conflicts with which he was engaged vis-à-vis his Lord.

This is, of course, assuming it was a *sane* " blik." However, the sudden unanticipated introduction of a religious solution to a strictly secular conflict violates the paradigm and suggests that the " blik " – far from setting one free in terms of the paradigm – is apt to obscure his conflict because his despair is made unconscious by the apparently satisfactory religious solution.

As an example, a woman of my acquaintance was struggling with a marital problem in which her husband threatened desertion. Rather abruptly she became deeply concerned with immortality and saw in the answers to this question the solution to all her problems. This " blik " must be regarded as an illusion and of a different psychological order than, say Peter's; the paradigm makes this conclusion inevitable. If such a distinction is not made, van Buren's "blikmanship" leads us only into greater confusion rather than clarity.

Moreover, the consequences are not spelled out. According to the paradigm's version of freedom, the image restores one's capacity to think empirically and to discern "meaning." By van Buren's notion of freedom, the "blik" sets one free "to be for others." But without a distinction between a sane and an insane "blik," van Buren must sanction consequences like those in the case of "Oscar."[4] Oscar's "blik" was essentially that he saw himself as Jesus; one may even say he saw Jesus "in a *new* way," and he decided that Jesus' freedom to die was his also. But he did not die for himself, he died "for others." He said:

> Something said to me, "Are you willing to commit suicide?" And it was just like I had to do it. I turned on the gas. That was for my wife. Then I slashed my wrists, one for one daughter and the other for the other daughter.

Quite literally, Oscar was free to be "for others" because he had discerned in Jesus something he wanted to imitate. However, according to the paradigm, Oscar's "freedom" was a form of religious pathology. Throughout his symptomatology he *had* to perform the bizarre acts; the predominant compulsion in itself indicates rigidity and the loss of freedom; but more significantly, Oscar lost touch with the empirical reality around him. Everything became not what it in social and empirical fact was but, rather, what it symbolized regarding his unique identification with Jesus. Thus "meaning," or interpretation, was lost as a separate mode capable of "balancing" the others, and it was fused into the image creating not meaning but an overwhelming sense of "ought."

On the other hand, it must be argued that for instance, Joan of Arc's " voices " may *not* have been pathological in the sense of the paradigm because they gave her vast insights into political and military reality. Her interpretations were brilliant; her freedom may have been actual and full according to the paradigm even though the auditory images were as bizarre as Oscar's. In opposition to this, one might object by mentioning dictators and tyrants who were also military and political geniuses. However, in such instances the earlier aspects of the paradigm would call other factors into question. For example, from Erik Erikson's analysis of Adolf Hitler [5] it is evident that certain developmental conflicts preoccupied Hitler throughout his life; his massive schemes were delusional in that they did not solve – in the sense of " relieve " – the conflicts. The point is that bizarre behavior in itself may perfectly well be an aspect of freedom according to the paradigm, provided the interpretative and empirical modes are not distorted.

Many of van Buren's formulations are very helpful, but the propaedeutics and the consequences of the " blik " need to be spelled out; otherwise they conjure too much and specify too little.

Consequences for Ethics

To continue the matter of spelling out consequences, the ethical upshot of the paradigm is essentially in agreement with the sort of contextual emphasis one finds in Paul Lehmann's volume *Ethics in a Christian Context.* Basically, the paradigm is not an ethical principle but, rather, an epistemological pattern. However, this epistemology is at the heart of Lehmann's concern because the paradigm spells out a version of mature humanity which is capable of participating in a " mature " community. Lehmann's use of " conscience " is not radically different from reality consciousness as it has been spelled out here, though he views it as constantly encountering what has here been described as " the flaw." Such a constant engagement with " ought " borders on pathological religiousness. Though Lehmann's preoccupation with this is justified in a book on ethics, one wonders if the freedom he describes ever really moves beyond a state of ethical conflict in spite of his claim that the human factor, not the " ought " factor, is the primary ethical reality.

However, the major problem that the paradigm poses to Lehmann's position is at the point of his epistemology. The paradigm is in essential agreement with Lehmann's view (taken from Richard Kroner, *The Religious Function of Imagination* [Yale University Press, 1941]) that the imagination of the Biblical writers subserves the revelation of God and " is the vehicle of that revelation." However, Lehmann fails to see, for all his understanding of contextualism, that paradigmatic, freedom-producing imagery is bound to the conflict which it was created to resolve. For *that* conflict and *those* writers it was decisive that it be expressed in the fashion in which it appeared. To take political imagery out of its context and emphasize " messianism " is — by the standard of the paradigm — removing the contextual decisiveness of the image and setting it up as a covert moralism of images to which one is called to conform, i.e., pictures have been substituted for precepts. This is, of course, not consistent with Lehmann's basic intentions, nor is it quite what Kroner had in mind. The problem is that there is an unclear epistemological formulation at the crux of Lehmann's argument.

The hypnagogic paradigm asserts that Biblical language and images become significant for freedom only when they become an indigenous part of one's life struggle in his body-environment matrix. But consistent with paradigmatic freedom, the Biblical language and imagery are most effective as factors in a preconscious belief about reality. Regardless of how bizarre the belief, if it restores one to empirical and interpretative relatedness to the world and for " true community," then the Biblical imagery has become effective. In this sense the whole point of the matter is indeed to make and keep life " truly human " (Lehmann) when conscious human existence is interpreted according to the paradigm. If one assumes that the distilled essence of Biblical imagery contains a truth to be imitated, then there is no epistemological difference between the grasp of the image and the grasp of a moral precept. Yet for Lehmann the consequences are supposed to be different: in the first, one subordinates the " ought " to the truly human; in the second, one reverses that priority. For conscious human experience, that could be the difference between pathology and freedom.

From the viewpoint of the paradigm, in order to keep the consequences straight, one must keep the epistemological conditions straight. For the Biblical narrative as for the present situation, the existing conflicts, from personal developmental ones to broad social, political, and technological problems, are epistemologically prior to any superordinate imagery which points to them. That is to say, ethics from the standpoint of the paradigm invites a full-fledged engagement with such issues, permitting solutions to arise anew as the imagination of this age subserves revelation in a manner analogous to its subservience in the Biblical narratives. We get from Biblical history a functional, not a substantive, analysis of the potential significance of paradigmatic freedom. According to the paradigm, one must move from the actual present in all dimensions of the body-environment matrix through the imagination and back into the matrix anew; the " finite " must be available down to the last inch if the future is not to be an illusion carved out of Biblical phraseology.

This is not to assert a basic disagreement with Lehmann's intentions, but to point to a deficiency in his position at a crucial juncture. The "mature humanity" is clearly derivative from the "truly human" in Jesus Christ; but how is he present in a fashion that does not capitulate to Biblical "iconography?" Or, in Kierkegaard's phrase, what is the "how" of the proclamation? Or to return to the words of the introductory chapter, What is the proximate psychic form of man that corresponds to the ultimate form of man in Jesus? The paradigm is a functional answer to this question. Moreover, since significant substance is only logically separable from the functional process by which it is created, and since significant substance is always unique, a functional answer may be the only one that can be given.

Thus, the paradigm suggests a corrective to Lehmann's viewpoint at the epistemological juncture; it does not attempt to propose the paradigm as the new precept. The paradigm in the final analysis is, like Lehmann's, "truly human": it is "given" serendipitously, perhaps fragmentarily, perhaps all at once, in a Moment. However, it goes somewhat farther: not only does it describe how the bestowal of a notion as bizarre as the Absolute Paradox can be known with conflict-resolving significance and at the same time set one firmly into the actualities of history, but also it describes how, through the perversity of its aspects, history may be symbolized, chinked with illusions, and — in modified forms — delusionally reconstructed. To be free for the present conflicts in whatever dimension of existence — predominant for whatever mode of consciousness — is to be free indeed; any specific imagery which sacralizes this freedom does not strengthen but, rather, perverts it.

CHAPTER

XI

RAMIFICATIONS OF THE PARADIGM: II

Interdisciplinary Studies

The problems in correlating concepts across disciplinary boundaries have, of course, been approached many times before.

One approach to these problems has been to make a sharp initial distinction between " faith " and " reason," then to carry this distinction into the study of psychology and make an analogous distinction between " philosophical " and " scientific " psychology. This characteristically Roman Catholic approach emulates the Thomistic tradition asserting that there can be no conflict between reason and faith; so it allows scientific psychology full autonomy, and it coordinates philosophical psychology with the superior transcendent knowledge of faith.

H. Misiak and V. M. Staudt, *Catholics in Psychology* (McGraw-Hill Book Company, Inc., 1954), carry out this argument most ably. Also, a clear-cut illustration of this method is the work by Pierre Teilhard de Chardin, *The Phenomenon of Man* (Harper & Brothers, 1959). A non-Catholic treatment, which is methodologically similar to the Thomistic ideal in the sense that no essential conflict is seen between religion and psychiatry, is Louis Linn and Leo W. Schwarz, *Psychiatry and Religious Experience*

(Random House, Inc., 1958).

The analytical method and the conclusions of the position stated in the foregoing chapters have attempted to avoid this essentially hylomorphic set of assumptions. It has asserted largely in keeping with Kierkegaard that faith is a creative fusion of psychic behavior and divine revelation, and it has attempted to assert that the paradigm describes the functional pattern of psychic life under the impact of divine revelation. As a result, the paradigm and its parody in pathological religiousness bound a spectrum composed of qualitatively distinct segments that are bridged in both directions by the creative acts of consciousness. Consequently, it has asserted that there is no feasible way to distinguish between faith and reason. Every act of consciousness is an imaginative integration of the condition which underlies it with the reasoning and memories which preceded it; the " belief " that is created is both a product of and catalyst for reasoning. The distinctions that can be made are functional, vis-à-vis relatively full paradigmatic freedom on the one hand, or illusory freedom on the other.

Another approach has taken the form of a reductionism in which one field simply subordinates the other to a category in which it can be summarily treated and dismissed. A type of religious reductionism is that which claims that the truly valuable psychiatric concepts are already present in the Scriptures, and they need only to be translated into that language in order for the initial *rapprochement* to take place between the two fields. This is often handled in too facile a way by fundamentalist groups, but an astute and insightful treatment is Otto A. Piper's volume *The Christian Interpretation of Sex* (Charles Scribner's Sons, 1955).

On the other hand, psychological reductionism is characterized by the relegation of all religious experience to categories of defensive or compensatory behavior which would be abandoned if it were understood in terms of the psychological realities that underlie it. Such writers as Erich Fromm, *Man for Himself* (Rinehart & Company, Inc., 1947), and *Psychoanalysis and Religion* (Yale University Press, 1950) – to mention some of his most explicit statements; and Otto Rank, *The Myth of the Birth of the Hero,* tr. by F. Robbins and Smith Ely Jelliffe (Journal of Nervous and Mental Disease Publishing Company, 1952); and Theodor Reik, *Mystery on the Mountain* (Harper & Brothers, 1959), have carried out this approach within their respective Freudian or neo-Freudian understandings of man. C. G. Jung's views may also be included schematically in this category. Though he is careful to qualify his religious viewpoints, acknowledging that psychic reality may not be able fully to explain religious reality, he nevertheless undertakes to construct an archetypal system which so completely exhausts the origins of religious experience that religious realities are left with almost nothing to explain and very little intrinsic worth. (See *Psychology and Religion* [Yale University Press, 1938]; *Answer to Job* [London: Routledge and Kegan Paul, Ltd., 1958].)

Either reductionistic approach involves the absorption of all the levels of understanding in one field into a portion of the other, with the result that only one of the two fields is necessary. From the outset this volume has attempted to eschew reductionism of either sort, believing that on both sides there is a cryptic assumption of verbal realism. Biblical reductionism assumes that Scriptural language is not only true but utterance of it is evidence of a correlative internal, behavioral truth; the language takes on a magical quality and is thereby not evidence of truth but of despair. Piper's volume is an exception to the strict meaning of this criticism, but his analysis does suggest that Biblical language exhausts all wisdom on the matter of sexuality, and he thereby precludes the possibility that, by virtue of the paradigm, Biblical wisdom may receive radically new significance. To preclude the paradigm on these grounds is to assert that all of behavior is to be evaluated by one of its aspects, namely, the correct use of correct language; in effect, language is more real than any other form of behavior.

On the other hand, psychiatric studies of religion have tended to be confined to the types of religious behavior that held to some form of verbal realism. Such an assumption made reductionism a necessity: the Biblically-minded verbal realist, while attempting to assert in effect that the validation of behavior can be reduced to language, has actually forced language into the service of his own anxiety. As was mentioned in Chapter III, since Freud rarely examined religious behavior apart from the basic analogy between it and pathology, it is not surprising that his followers made the same error.

The paradigm has attempted to move beyond this standoff at the level of verbal realism and to assert that language is always tinged with the coloring of an imaginative background which never emerges explicitly in the grammatical forms or meanings that it conveys. Therefore, it cannot exhaust behavioral truth. But more than that, according to the paradigm, language affects preconscious imagery by structuring the conflicts that will be resolved by the ensuing image. Since the image can solve only the conflicts that are set before it, language is determinative to the extent that the "material" images (e.g., Silberer's image of "transsubjective" values) that appear in hypnagogic phenomena are in part dependent upon verbal forms to construct a problem. Moreover, a certain portion of one's internalized view of reality is directly linked to verbal symbols; accordingly, an aspect of all "judgments" about reality are shaped by linguistic phenomena. Seen in this light, language figures sometimes decisively, sometimes incidentally, into the imaginative work of consciousness; but the richness, complexity, and symbolic value of the image are always beyond the limits that verbal forms can encompass. It is evident, therefore, that verbal forms are deficient in their capacity to establish the boundaries of paradigmatic freedom. Moreover, the attempt to evaluate religious experience either positively or negatively by means of its verbal assertions is at best an ecclesiastical or psychiatric convenience, fundamentally deficient in its understanding of the function that language serves in the paradigm of reality consciousness.

Carl Jung was cited above as a possible exception to the criticism stated here; surely his analyses of the dynamics of religious behavior are not as intentionally reductionistic as Freud's, and his emphasis upon creative imagery is surely in keeping with the hypnagogic paradigm. However, he has created a psychic basement furnished with archetypal antiques to account for the analogical continuities he finds among persons, races, and generations. This is a fascinating but seemingly unnecessary set of constructs for the analysis of consciousness; if creativity and continuity in psychic life can be accounted for without such semimystical notions, it seems to violate the principles of parsimony to invoke them. Moreover, paradigmatic religious experience is predominantly concerned with conscious functioning and historical actualities, not with the replacement of metaphysics by metapsychology.

A third approach is to construct a *tertium quid* in which the two disciplines can find a common parlance that will interpret the language of one to the language of the other. This approach characteristically utilizes philosophical language and method. It is an approach that is particularly adaptable to modes of ontological analysis. Paul Tillich's methodological position is the most significant adherent to the *tertium quid* approach. His methodology emerges from an ontology in which the distinction between essence and existence is decisive. For him, ontology is the bridge between the disciplines which have " preliminary concerns " and theology which has " ultimate concerns." [1] However, this approach has the questionable consequence of relegating both fields of understanding to a position of irrelevance with respect to ontological structures of analysis. The approach then takes on the appearance of a reductionism in favor of the third realm of discourse, the philosophical system itself.

Formulation of the paradigm has been made through an analysis of functional analogies that existed between two historically significant and systematically conceived viewpoints. The goal has been to reach a description of reality consciousness as a pattern of functioning. Ontological questions per se have been largely left aside not only in order to avoid a philosophical reductionism but also to avoid irrelevance to ontic phenomena.

However, ontology has come into the discussion decisively at one point: Kierkegaard asserted that the Absolute Paradox was an ontological reality. The paradigm declares that ontological statements are possible because there are " ultimate " limits to which consciousness can " expand." (The strict ontologist would reverse the priority and assert that this, of course, would be the ontology of consciousness.) Thus, the distinction between " preliminary " and " ultimate " concern is made possible by the ability of the imagination to reconstruct the conditions under which consciousness is expanded to its limit (positively as " freedom " and negatively as " despair ") and withdrawn therefrom. Of such are the epistemological grounds of " ultimate " and " proximate " respectively.

The paradigm suggests constructively for Tillichian categories an epistemological differentiation of the vagary "participation." In his distinction between symbol and sign, Tillich asserts that signs are arbitrary in what they designate; symbols, on the other hand, "participate" in that to which they point. By this differentiation, words, as described by the paradigm, are generally signs, but imagery is at the level of the symbolic. To the extent that the God-man is verbal and conceptual he is a sign, but when he is "bestowed" he becomes a symbol in that he participates in the reality consciousness – indeed, in the true humanity – of which he was first but a sign. It is in this sense that the God-man is an ontological category; as a verbal structure he is a sign (to continue with Tillich's distinction) of the ontological possibility of paradigmatic freedom which, when it is bestowed, converts the God-man from a sign into a symbol. The consequent freedom, then, not only validates itself but also the ontological reality to which the God-man pointed. The epistemological differentiation of this possibility is what the paradigm describes.

However, because individual versions of the symbol of the God-man vary as do personal images of the "ultimate," the God-man is "believed" to the extent that he is a symbol and not a sign; nevertheless, he is posited as pointing to an ontological reality. This "positing" is made not out of pure subjectivity but out of the freedom to enter fully into empirical historical reality, to engage in social conflict for the sake of meaning and to entertain both corporate and solitary joy.

While this may seem to be saying that the validity of the freedom is to be judged by its consequences, it is not. The characteristics of pathological religiousness (Chapter IV) are indications of the absence of reality consciousness, but with many substantive variations these become popular patterns of behavior, i.e., religious systems in the broadest sense. Thus the paradigm cuts across social effectiveness asserting that it is deficient as a criterion for reality consciousness. On the other hand, it cuts across stereotypical distinctions between sanity and insanity, not as the "blik" on grounds of ignorance about subjective attitudes, but on the grounds that bizarre behavior – even so-called mental illness – may be instrumental in the creation of a full grasp of the empirical. Moreover, an individual's "different" religious language may be expressive of reality consciousness whereas "common sense" may be expressive merely of a corporate pathology. Thus reality consciousness is "ultimately" self-validating, but it is able to be differentiated in terms of its functions in the four modalities and in terms of their mutually corrective character. This functional analysis is for the individual a retrospective description – or we may even say, a phenomenology – of the measure of freedom that has been "given."

To summarize, the paradigm is an epistemological model of conscious functioning that describes how an ontological reality such as the God-man, which makes claims upon human consciousness, is known, not in itself only, but also in terms of its claims. By this line of reasoning, the correlation between the systematic viewpoints of Freud and Kierkegaard has not reduced ontology to epistemology, nor has the reverse error suggested by the *tertium quid* approach been committed.

Education and the Paradigm

The pernicious distinction that has been ruinous to a great deal of theoretical thinking about Christian education lies between content and process. One of the unique disservices that Barthiana did for Christian education was to precipitate radical opposition to the Christian appropriations of John Dewey's thought. The polarities have become so stereotyped that one might argue the reverse positions with no less distortion. That is, Karl Barth's dialectics in theology comprise a functional analysis of the use of theological language, whereas John Dewey's emphasis upon finding solutions to problems was really content-centered. The point is that the distinction is false and misleading not only for the act of teaching and learning but also in terms of the chief proponents on the two sides of the opposition.

The paradigm asserts that the aim of education is expansion of the boundaries of paradigmatic freedom. Moreover, it asserts that paradigmatic freedom is a fusion of content and process; indeed, it is precisely in the fusion that consciousness is created. At their origins Biblical knowledge and creedal formulations are the creative resolutions to psychological, sociological, and cultural conflicts of the eras in which they appeared. Strangely, yet logically enough, that is precisely how they are learned today, i.e., as solutions to current issues, but the intention behind their contemporary appropriation is nothing like the intentions that created them in the first place. Both intentions are valid, but their identity can never be assumed; each " meaning " is extracted from a different body-environment matrix.

The consciousness of contemporary persons in the prepuberty years is shaped by those factors which resolve their psychosocial and cultural conflicts; the predominant issues in their lives, no matter how rationalized the issues may be, concern first their place in the family (or the absence of a family) and eventually their place among their peers. Perhaps the clearest, if also a bit too artistically abstract, formulation of these developmental conflicts is presented in Erik Erikson's recently revised *Childhood and Society*. From the developmental standpoint, the eight epigenetically related stages of life [2] that he formulates are designated by decisive crises or conflicts at a psychosocial level. The paradigm would declare that failure to cope successfully with these crises tends to precipitate the patterns of pathological religiousness; success of the imagination in resolving these conflicts is developmental movement in the direction of reality consciousness.

The role of Biblical and creedal knowledge per se in the prepuberty process of maturation is great or little, depending on how well it enables the parent to establish support and appropriate limits for the child in his facing of the life crises. There is no straightforward verbal method by which Biblical or creedal truth can be conveyed; the language is "meaningful" or fantastic (of private worth only to the parent) according to the attitudinal interrelationship of the parent and the child. Either the Biblical language contributes to the articulation of what the child's imagination has already created according to the dynamics of the paradigm in reaction to the developmental crises, or it is learned strictly as an expedience to reduce the immediate tension of being told to learn something. The latter, of course, contributes minimally to the expansion of the boundaries of freedom.

For instance, in the period when the child's crisis concerns the alternatives of autonomy versus shame and doubt, the decisive matter is whether the parents are sensitive to and able to support the child's autonomy. Talk to the child about God's loving him as he is may be meaningful, but talk to him about giving himself to God can only have a negative effect – if any at all – since giving himself up is precisely the opposite of the emergent movement of freedom in his life toward autonomy. Eventually – particularly in puberty – the whole story of David's shame over Bathsheba and God's forgiveness will successfully or unsuccessfully articulate one's image of shame-versus-autonomy depending largely upon how the problem of autonomy was worked through during the earlier years of his life. On the other hand, the Biblical or theological differentiation of the image of autonomy cannot be made unless appropriate words and grammar have been learned. Moreover, because interpretations are contingent upon the structures of problems, the words and concepts cannot become definitive, even in puberty, unless it is through them that the issue is first constructed, i.e., the proper conflict framed. In effect, the paradigm applies developmentally as well as phenomenologically; or, may we say, paradigmatic freedom has a developmental dimension.

One of the major difficulties in the use of Erikson's views is his relatively light treatment of the role of language and cognition. For the prepuberty years his emphasis is correct, but at puberty what Jean Piaget calls " rational coordination " develops. At that time cognition becomes a decisive determinant, for now as never before the child can reflect upon his own thoughts from the vantage point of others. In effect, the full dimensions of empirical existence are open to him, for he can now *test* his conclusions, let us say, about natural reality; moreover, he can acquire the capacity for testing meaning against social actualities. In puberty for the first time the full scope of reality consciousness is a psychological possibility through the full development of cognitive patterns.

Thus, the communicant instruction of an adolescent which *requires* for " adulthood " (i.e., communicant membership) beliefs that defy the power of cognition is not only frustrating to the young person, but also it is ironically a truncation of paradigmatic freedom in the name of the true humanity; the paradigm would declare such instruction to be not only self-contradictory but also self-destructive. The paradigm suggests to the contrary that cognition, the power to test the empirical and to acquire cultural meanings, should be pushed to its limits in tension with Christian thought.[3]

While the young person's reality consciousness is stifled

if he must stop thinking to become a Christian adult, he is at the same time living in a psychosocial matrix in which he needs to find "fidelity" in order to acquire "identity" (Erikson's conceptualizations). This is to say, in puberty as never before, the resolution to the developmental crisis ("identity versus role confusion") will involve a complex psychosocial image in which language and cognition become decisive factors.

The general point is that the acquisition of meaning – ultimate or incidental – is a paradigmatic fusion of the body-environment matrix with the developmental conflicts of a particular period. Paradigmatic freedom in the full sense is not a possibility for the individual until the years of puberty. It may be well to note at this point that the case of Little Hans bears out well the fact that meanings must be added to the developmental struggle by one who has the capacity for rational coordinate thought (in Hans's case, Dr. Freud and the father) if the appropriate conflict is to be faced and resolved. When one retains this capacity within himself, then paradigmatic freedom can for him become self-validating. This is the aim of education for the mature years.

It was stated earlier in this section that the intentions lying behind Biblical material are to be distinguished from the intentions that create meaning for the contemporary learner. This proposition indicates that the paradigm includes the principle that not only Biblical but also doctrinal and ecclesiastical history is the creative resolution to the psychosocial and cultural conflicts which appeared in past eras. The research behind the teaching-learning act is most effectively tracing the course of the emergence of reality consciousness when it is reconstructing the crises for which the recorded event was the resultant meaning. According to the paradigm, one only knows what that "meaning" meant if he can trace it to its indigenous causes in a multidimensional conflict.

One of the most helpful studies contributing to such an understanding of crucial events is Erikson's study, *Young Man Luther*. One cannot argue that this psychosocial study is exhaustive, but the dimension it adds to the history of the Reformation is indispensable to an interpretation of the " meanings " of that period, which are resolutions to multilevel conflicts inherent in the so-called " events " of the Reformation. When the psychosocial and cultural matrix has been conceived, one may appreciate – yet not appropriate – the historical meanings accurately; appropriation remains a matter of contemporary conflict-resolution.

The assumption that content and process can be separated in the appropriation of meaning is delusional; valid meanings are repeatedly created anew for a total context and cannot, like objects, be carted intact from one sociocultural matrix to the next. Paradigmatically, then, Christian education is structuring the creative act for the purpose of expanding the boundaries of freedom. Without this central emphasis, it becomes fantastic, and in Kierkegaard's words: " Christian education is a lie."

This chapter has attempted to delineate the ramifications of the paradigm as it strikes at epistemological issues in theology, psychiatric theory, education, and related fields of inquiry. The paradigm has made it possible for psychiatric theory to recognize, within its own canons, not only the potential " sanity " in religious belief but also its uniqueness. It has enabled theological thinking to explore the " how " of the proclamation as well as the " how not " in the characteristic deformations of pathological religiousness. In setting these boundaries, the discussion has explored the phenomenological spectrum of consciousness and suggested the nature and significance of its developmental axis, thereby indicating that the boundaries of

Christian education theory are to be set by the demands of paradigmatic freedom.

The future of the paradigm lies in its being transactionally related to social theory, theological language, and institutional practice. The development of such a set of relationships might be conceived as a systematic approach to practical theology.

Notes

CHAPTER I. *Introduction:* OBJECTIONS TO WRITING THIS BOOK

1. The reader is here referred to the dissertation from which this book is derived: James E. Loder, "The Nature of Religious Consciousness in the Writings of Sigmund Freud and Søren Kierkegaard" (submitted to the Committee on Higher Degrees in the History and Philosophy of Religion, Harvard University, Cambridge, Massachusetts, April, 1962).

2. The use of "conscious" or "consciousness" may seem to raise an aging controversy about the usefulness of the term. (See William James, *The Principles of Psychology* [Dover Publications, 1950], Volume I, Chapters IX and X; Bertrand Russell, *The Analysis of Mind* [The Macmillan Company, 1921], especially Chapter I; Gilbert Ryle, *The Concept of Mind* [Barnes & Noble, Inc., 1949].) Clearly, the term will be used here with a meaning that will be refined out of the writings of Kierkegaard and Freud. If an apology were needed in order to justify resuscitation of the term "consciousness," it would be based upon the fact that consciousness is the major area in which both Kierkegaard and Freud have a phenomenological concern and to which both speak explicitly on a common level of understanding. As suggested above, an interdisciplinary analysis on a metaphysical or metapsychological level — on any level other than that of the phenomenology of consciousness — becomes a standoff or it capitulates immediately to a reductionistic fallacy.

CHAPTER II. *Pathological Religiousness:* KIERKEGAARD

1. Søren Kierkegaard, *The Point of View for My Work as an Author,* tr. by Walter Lowrie (London: Oxford University Press, 1939), p. 124.

2. Søren Kierkegaard, *Attack Upon "Christendom,"* tr. by Walter Lowrie (Princeton University Press, 1944), p. 30.

3. Søren Kierkegaard, *The Journals of Søren Kierkegaard,* a selection ed. and tr. by Alexander Dru (London: Oxford University Press, 1938), No. 614, p. 178.

It is worthy of notice that Kierkegaard is directing his criticism at the way in which Hegelian thought had influenced clerical (especially Bishop Martensen's) rationalization about the masses.

4. That Kierkegaard considers a man's submission to the crowd to be his status prior to his attainment of individual existence is evidenced by the priority given to an Aesthetic sphere of existence in *Stages on Life's Way,* Hilarius Bookbinder (Søren Kierkegaard), tr. by Walter Lowrie (Princeton University Press, 1940); and *Concluding Unscientific Postscript* to the "Philosophical Fragments," Johannes Climacus (Søren Kierkegaard), tr. by David F. Swenson and Walter Lowrie (Princeton University Press, for the American-Scandinavian Foundation, 1941). That is, achievement of "existential reality" presupposes adult social involvement.

5. Kierkegaard, *The Journals,* No. 614, p. 178.

6. Kierkegaard, *Point of View,* p. 162.

7. *Ibid.,* pp. 97 and 41 ff.

8. Johannes Climacus (Søren Kierkegaard), *Philosophical Fragments or a Fragment of Philosophy,* tr. by David F. Swenson (Princeton University Press, 1936), p. 66.

9. Kierkegaard, *Postscript,* p. 347.

10. For future reference to this use of "words" in Kierkegaard's writing, direct communication must be distinguished from "indirect communication." The latter refers to the idea doubly reflected in more advanced stages of existence. In the Aesthetic Stage of existence the "word" is not intended to be doubly reflected. Rather, to him who has only an Aesthetic ex-

istence, the word is intended to convey a feeling directly, that is, when it is reflected upon but once.

11. Victor Eremita (Søren Kierkegaard), *Either/Or: A Fragment of Life,* Vol. I, tr. by David F. Swenson and Lillian Marvin Swenson (Princeton University Press, 1944).

12. Kierkegaard, *Postscript,* p. 347.

13. It should be evident how Hegel's System fits into the Aesthetic pattern. In the quotation above (see note 10) the "Idea" refers to the "Notion" or "Idea" in Hegelian thought, as well as to the psychological phenomenon.

14. Classical behaviorists (J. B. Watson) as well as neo-behaviorists (B. F. Skinner) have uncritically adopted the line of argument that what exists, exists in some quantity; it can therefore be measured and controlled. This line of thought which leads directly from a quantitative analysis of human behavior to its manipulability is at work here; Kierkegaard's position has argued that this is an illusory view of human nature.

15. Vigilius Haufniensis (Søren Kierkegaard), *The Concept of Dread,* tr. by Walter Lowrie (Princeton University Press, 1944), p. 38.

16. *Ibid.,* p. 45.

17. *Ibid.*

18. *Ibid.*

19. *Ibid.,* p. 55.

20. *Ibid.,* p. 97.

21. *Ibid.*

22. Anti-Climacus (Søren Kierkegaard), *The Sickness Unto Death,* tr. by Walter Lowrie (A Doubleday Anchor Book, 1954), p. 182.

23. *Ibid.,* p. 201.

24. *Ibid.,* p. 203.

25. *Ibid.,* p. 147.

26. *Ibid.*

27. *Ibid.,* pp. 272–273.

CHAPTER III. *Pathological Religiousness:* THE FREUDIAN DIMENSION I

1. Sigmund Freud, *Psychopathology of Everyday Life*, tr. by James Strachey in *The Standard Edition of the Complete Psychological Works of Sigmund Freud* (London: Hogarth Press, Ltd., and The Institute of Psychoanalysis, 1960), Vol. VI, pp. 258–259.

2. In *An Autobiographical Study* (W. W. Norton & Company, Inc., 1935), p. 138, Freud wrote, "I perceived ever more clearly that the events of human history, the interactions between human nature, cultural development and the precipitates of primaeval experiences (the most prominent example of which is religion) are no more than a reflection of the dynamic conflicts between the ego, the id, and the super-ego, which psychoanalysis studies in the individual – are the very same processes repeated upon a wider stage."

3. Sigmund Freud, *Obsessive Acts and Religious Practices, Collected Papers*, tr. by Joan Riviere (London: Hogarth Press, Ltd., 1924), Vol. II, pp. 30–35.

4. This formalized relationship, which is intended to encompass the totality of Freud's views of reality testing, has been described by Robert Waelder, *The International Journal of Psychoanalysis* (London: Baillière, Tindall & Cox, Ltd., 1936), Vol. XVII, pp. 92 f.

5. The particular meaning of "belief" which is intended here may be found in *The Origins of Psychoanalysis*, tr. by Eric Mosbacher and James Strachey (Basic Books, Inc., 1954), pp. 394–395. It is sufficient to say here that it is not to be equated with religious belief, but is rather an unverifiable conviction about external reality.

6. This is the Freudian category suggested by Waelder, (*loc. cit.*), as the most precise and most inclusive of these intrapsychic influences as they impinge upon and are understood and utilized by consciousness.

7. Sigmund Freud, *Introductory Lectures on Psychoanalysis*, tr. by Joan Riviere (London: George Allen & Unwin, Ltd., n.d.), p. 220.

8. Sigmund Freud, *The Ego and the Id,* ed. by James Strachey and tr. by Joan Riviere (W. W. Norton & Company, Inc., 1961), p. 69n1.

9. Waelder, *loc. cit.*, p. 92.

10. Freud, *Collected Papers,* Vol. II, p. 277.

11. *Ibid.*, p. 279.

12. Freud, *The Ego and the Id,* p. 76.

13. Sigmund Freud, *The Problem of Anxiety,* tr. by James Strachey (The Psychoanalytic Quarterly Press and W. W. Norton & Company, Inc., 1936), p. 80.

14. Sigmund Freud, *New Introductory Lectures on Psychoanalysis* (W. W. Norton & Company, Inc., 1933), p. 117.

15. Freud, *Standard Edition,* Vol. X, p. 241.

16. *Ibid.*, p. 244.

17. *Ibid.*

18. *Ibid.*, p. 247.

19. *Ibid.*, pp. 158 f.

20. In connection with "isolation" Freud also discusses "undoing," but the latter is described almost exclusively from the standpoint of motor activity, and this will not be of particular value to the understanding of obsessional neurosis, which is being interpreted here largely from an endopsychic standpoint. However, the symbolic manipulation of the external world, including the body of the subject, is further evidence of the unusual fashion in which images are juxtaposed in order to construct the neurotic's view of reality.

21. Freud, *Standard Edition,* Vol. X, p. 121.

CHAPTER IV. *Pathological Religiousness:* THE FREUDIAN DIMENSION II

1. Freud, *Standard Edition,* Vol. XI, p. 123.

2. It is provocative to realize that religionists knew the personal population of heaven long before Freud discovered his prototype in the human mind. Since Freud's dualistic view of the psyche is so perfectly analogous to the basic religious dualism, it seems possible that the central content of the unconscious may have been dictated by religion rather than the other way around. This, which is the exact reverse of Freud's asser-

tion, is the viewpoint of Karl Barth stated in so many words in *Prayer: According to the Catechisms of the Reformation,* tr. by Sara F. Terrien (The Westminster Press, 1952), pp. 33–36.

3. Sigmund Freud, *Totem and Taboo,* tr. by James Strachey (W. W. Norton & Company, Inc., 1952).

4. Freud, *Standard Edition,* Vol. XVII, p. 262.

5. Freud, *Totem and Taboo,* p. 132.

6. *Ibid.,* p. 144.

7. *Ibid.,* p. 145.

8. *Ibid.*

9. *Ibid.,* p. 158.

10. Of course, Freud has prepared the way for this in *The Interpretation of Dreams* (tr. by A. A. Brill [Random House, Inc., 1950]), which taught that analogy was one of the chief ways in which unconscious thought was translated into conscious thought.

11. Sigmund Freud, *The Future of an Illusion* (A Doubleday Anchor Book, 1957), pp. 52–54.

12. *Ibid.,* pp. 77–78.

13. *Ibid.,* pp. 88–89.

14. Sigmund Freud, *Moses and Monotheism,* tr. by Katherine Jones (London: Hogarth Press, Ltd., 1939), p. 204.

15. *Ibid.,* p. 139.

16. Sigmund Freud, *Group Psychology and the Analysis of the Ego,* tr. by James Strachey (Liveright Pub. Corp., 1922), pp. 113–115.

17. *Ibid.,* p. 141.

CHAPTER V. *Reality Becomes Conscious:* KIERKEGAARD

1. Kierkegaard, *Postscript,* p. 68.

2. *Ibid.,* p. 100.

3. *Ibid.,* p. 107.

4. Kierkegaard, *Sickness Unto Death,* p. 146.

5. Kierkegaard, *Philosophical Fragments,* p. 29.

6. *Ibid.,* p. 37.

7. Kierkegaard, *Sickness Unto Death,* p. 147.

8. Kierkegaard, *Postscript,* p. 507.

9. *Ibid.*

10. *Ibid.*, p. 508.
11. *Ibid.*
12. This is a double-pronged attack by Kierkegaard: one against Hegel who conceptualized man as a synthesis of the finite and the infinite and the other against Socrates who believed, according to Plato's presentation, in the reincarnation of souls and the doctrine of recollection.
13. This is Kierkegaard's term for the renewed relationship which an individual in Paradoxical Religiousness has to his spatiotemporal environment. It is of special significance because of the relationship to Aesthetic existence that it suggests.
14. Søren Kierkegaard, *The Journals,* No. 633, p. 194.
15. In 1849, the same year in which *Sickness Unto Death* was published, Søren Kierkegaard wrote in his *Journals* (No. 1002) that reality was the enemy of the imagination. "When it is a matter of understanding (something) in reality I am relieved of any *effort* of the imagination." This summarizes an opinion expounded at length in *Repetition: An Essay in Experimental Psychology,* Constantine Constantius (Søren Kierkegaard), tr. by Walter Lowrie (Princeton University Press, 1952), and to some extent in *Either/Or*. It is a clear indication of the close relationship between transparency and reality, and of the absence of any *deceit* of the imagination in that relationship.
16. This historical relativity is most extensively expounded in the *Philosophical Fragments* and in Book One, Chapter I, of *Concluding Unscientific Postscript.*
17. Kierkegaard, *Philosophical Fragments,* pp. 35 f.
18. *Ibid.*, p. 42.
19. *Ibid.*, p. 50.
20. In *The Journals,* Søren Kierkegaard says, "Faith . . . implies an act of will," but this seems to contradict his direct assertion in the *Philosophical Fragments,* "Faith is not an act of will." These may be reconciled by an interpretation of "implies" as referring to the stages preceding Religiousness A. However, if it be insisted that the contradiction should prevail, surely the latter is more representative of Søren Kierkegaard's view, for it occurs at a central point in a major writing, and it

was written later than the first statement by ten years (1834–1844). Finally, it is more consistent with the dialectical development of his thought and the uniqueness of the "Moment."

21. Hermann Diem, *Kierkegaard's Dialectic of Existence*, tr. by H. Knight (Edinburgh: Oliver & Boyd, Ltd., 1959), p. 48.

22. Kierkegaard, *The Journals*, No. 207, p. 59.

23. Kierkegaard, *Postscript*, p. 535n.

24. Kierkegaard, *The Journals*, No. 661, p. 206.

25. This Apostolic state is exemplified also in Kierkegaard's extended treatment of the "Knight of Faith" in Johannes de Silentio, *Fear and Trembling: A Dialectical Lyric*, tr. by Walter Lowrie (A Doubleday Anchor Book, 1954). The Knight constantly makes his movement into faith by virtue of the absurd, i.e., by understanding the Paradox as a category, and "yet in such a way, be it observed, that [he] does not lose the finite but gains it every inch" (p. 48).

26. This distinction between the metaphysical or metapsychological level of understanding and the phenomenological or descriptive level is not as important in the analysis of each thinker's own system of concepts as it is in the process of correlation between two systems. Since this study is concerned with the correlation of concepts, the distinction has been made here, indicating that the primary emphasis in the foregoing discussion of Kierkegaard's writings has been upon understanding his position from the standpoint of the latter level.

CHAPTER VI. *Consciousness as Reality:* FREUD

1. Ernest Jones, *The Life and Work of Sigmund Freud* (Basic Books, 1953), Vol. II, p. 313.

2. Freud, *Psychopathology of Everyday Life* in *Standard Edition*, Vol. XII, pp. 215 f.

3. *Ibid.*, "Editor's Note," pp. 215–216.

4. *Ibid.*, p. 216.

5. Freud, *The Interpretation of Dreams*, p. 463.

6. *Ibid.*, p. 470.

7. *Ibid.*, pp. 463, 467.

8. Freud, *Standard Edition*, Vol. XIV, p. 171. Freud's indebtedness to Kant on these points is made explicit here. As

Ernest Jones has pointed out (*op. Cit.*, Vol. I), the single philosophical mind that had the most direct informative influence on Freud was that of Franz Brentano. More will be said about Brentano's influence at a later point. It may be noted that what Freud attributes here to Kant is also one of the major philosophical assumptions that lie behind the contributions of Brentano to the psychology of perception (Gardner Murphy, *Historical Introduction to Modern Psychology* (Harcourt, Brace & Co., Inc., 1949), p. 235.

9. Freud, *Standard Edition,* Vol. XII, p. 219.

10. *Ibid.*

11. The "economic" understanding of the personality was not stated formally by Freud until 1915. This statement points out that the conceptual pattern which Freud was using here already included what he later termed "economic": "This point of view endeavors to follow out the vicissitudes of amounts of excitation and to arrive at least at some relative estimate of their magnitude" (*Standard Edition,* Vol. XIV, p. 181).

12. Freud, "Two Principles of Mental Functioning," *Standard Edition,* Vol. XII, p. 223.

13. This differentiation of consciousness is explicated in brief in the "Two Principles of Mental Functioning," but is more extensively treated in "The Project for a Scientific Psychology," *The Origins of Psychoanalysis,* especially p. 418.

14. Thomas S. Szasz has given an acute conceptual analysis of this problem in his volume *Pain and Pleasure* (Basic Books, Inc., 1957). Although the concern of this discussion is only with the writings of Freud, it should be indicated that from Szasz's volume it is evident that a great deal of conceptual uncertainty arises from close study of these terms. Thus establishing their meaning in the context of Freud's libido theory is not a solution to the broader, more complex issue of whether to conceptualize pleasure and pain as psychogenic, somatogenic, or as some fusion of the two sources in a sociological setting.

15. Freud, "The Project," *The Origins of Psychoanalysis,* p. 380.

16. Freud, *The Interpretation of Dreams,* p. 466.

17. Freud, "The Project," *The Origins of Psychoanalysis,* pp. 366–372.

18. Freud, *The Interpretation of Dreams,* p. 464.

19. Sigmund Freud, *Three Contributions to the Theory of Sex,* in *The Basic Writings of Sigmund Freud,* ed. and tr. by A. A. Brill (Random House, Inc., 1938), p. 611.

20. *Ibid.*

21. Freud, *On Narcissism,* in *Standard Edition,* Vol. XIV, p. 75.

22. *Ibid.,* p. 84.

23. This general line of argument has also been suggested by Bartlett H. Stoodley, *The Concepts of Sigmund Freud* (The Free Press of Glencoe, 1959), especially Chapters VIII and IX.

24. Freud, *Beyond the Pleasure Principle* (1920), in *Standard Edition,* Vol. XVIII, pp. 7–8.

25. The term "bound" is to be understood here as: bound to secondary process functions. Unbound excitation is recognized intrapsychically as "impulses arising from instincts," as "freely mobile processes which press toward discharge." Further reference to Freud's meaning for this term and its significance in Breuer's writings may be found in *The Origins of Psychoanalysis,* p. 425.

26. Freud makes this explicit in "Mourning and Melancholia," *Collected Papers,* Vol. IV.

27. Freud, *On Narcissism,* in *Standard Edition,* Vol. XIV, p. 85.

28. Freud, *Beyond the Pleasure Principle,* in *Standard Edition,* Vol. XVIII, p. 62. In this important theoretical writing Freud pointed out that the "pleasure principle seems actually to serve the death instincts" (p. 63). However, the buildup of tension is in fact a preliminary function that binds an instinctual impulse and prepares the excitation for its final elimination in the pleasure of discharge. By this pleasure derived from "expiring," Freud linked the pleasure principle closely with the death instinct.

29. As Strachey has noted, there is a rather long development through Freud's thought of the agency that is responsible for "reality testing." However, as will be noted in the follow-

ing paragraph, the refinements of Freud's views in this matter were largely on a metapsychological level; the formal relationship between observer and observed always remained the nucleus of how consciousness measured the reality of its relationships with the external world and with the forces of the primary process.

CHAPTER VII. THE STRUCTURAL SYNTHESIS

1. For Freud, the assertion being made here gains supplementary support from two sources: (*a*) Strachey has made the interesting, and perhaps very important, point that in *The Ego and the Id*, pp. 23 f., Freud uses two words, *bewusst sein* when writing of consciousness; he does not use the regular German word *Bewusstsein*. In its grammatical form *bewusst* is a passive participle, and the form used here is to be translated literally as "being conscioused." Since Freud's usage here is to be taken in the passive sense, it seems that the passive interpretation which this discussion has given to Freud's view of consciousness, i.e., its having no independent essence of its own, is corroborated by the very grammatical form of the term that Freud used to designate the phenomenon of consciousness. Strachey makes this grammatical observation in two other places: a footnote at the end of the Editor's Note to Freud's metapsychological paper on *The Unconscious* in *Standard Edition,* Vol. XIV, p. 165; an editorial footnote in Freud's paper, *The Question of Lay Analysis,* in *Standard Edition,* Vol. XX, p. 197. (*b*) Franz Brentano – Freud's early instructor in philosophy – accented this very point in the study of consciousness and accordingly may have had some influence upon Freud's later thinking. Brentano taught that the appropriate subject matter for psychological investigation is the act of perceiving or experiencing an object; to study consciousness apart from content, or the content of consciousness apart from the experience of it, was to make a false distinction and to be in error from the outset.

2. Kierkegaard, *Concluding Unscientific Postscript,* p. 100.

3. Freud, *An Autobiographical Study,* in *Standard Edition,* Vol. XX, pp. 58–59.

4. Sigmund Freud, *An Outline of Psychoanalysis,* tr. by James Strachey (W. W. Norton & Company, Inc., 1949), p. 37.

5. Freud, *The Ego and the Id,* p. 24.

6. This derivation can be examined more fully by consulting the methodological sections of the dissertation from which these pages are adapted.

7. George Santayana, *Dialogues in Limbo* (University of Michigan Press, 1957), p. 238.

Chapter VIII. *The Image:* CREATOR OF OBJECT AND MEANING

1. This description of the conditions for a psycho-logical relationship was suggested by Floyd H. Allport, *Theories of Perception and the Concept of Structure* (John Wiley & Sons, Inc., 1955), p. 120.

2. Kierkegaard, *Sickness Unto Death,* p. 164.

3. *Ibid.,* p. 273n4.

4. W. Windelband, *A History of Philosophy,* tr. by James H. Tufts (The Macmillan Company, 1950, copyright 1893), p. 580.

5. Johann Gottlieb Fichte, *The Vocation of Man,* tr. by William Smith (The Open Court Publishing Company, 1906), p. 89.

6. Kierkegaard, *The Journals,* No. 467, p. 128.

7. Kierkegaard, *Repetition,* p. 12.

8. *Ibid.*

9. Freud, "The Project," *The Origins of Psychoanalysis,* p. 395.

10. The word "image" is the English for the German *Bild.* This is significant because for the same category of phenomena Freud later uses *Vorstellung.* The latter word has greater flexibility and is used to include both the notion of a fixed pattern and its innervation; in this later usage it is perhaps best understood as "presentation." Thus in future references an "image" will always be referred to in direct relationship to its innervation, or the two aspects will be included in the one word, "presentation." Thereby, the dynamics implicit in Freud's thought will not be overlooked. Further reference to Freud's general usage of *Vorstellung* may be found in the

Standard Edition, Vol. XIV, p. 201n1.

11. Not an image *of* a relationship, which implies that a relationship exists apart from the image. Rather, it is precisely the image that binds functioning and subject matter in order to create consciousness.

12. The distinction being made here is very similar to a view of Brentano which, as already pointed out, had considerable influence on Freud's thinking regarding the "image." The nature of the influence is described succinctly in Gardner Murphy's account of Brentano's major concern in the revision of psychological inquiry. "Brentano held that the distinction is to be made between experience as a structure and the experience as a way of acting. For example, in the case of sensation there is a difference between the quality 'red' and the *sensing* of 'red.' The true subject-matter of psychology, said Brentano, is not, for example, 'red,' but the process of 'experiencing red,' the act which the mind carries out when it, so to speak, 'reddens.'" (Murphy, *op. cit.,* pp. 225–226.) The image, so to speak, "colors" consciousness in a particular fashion, and that coloring is then differentiated, or simply apprehended, depending on the mode of experiencing the "color," i.e., the mode of consciousness.

13. Freud, "The Project," *The Origins of Psychoanalysis.*

14. Freud, *Standard Edition,* Vol. II, p. 69.

15. The translation of this Latin phrase is literally "the form of all." However, when *instar* is followed by the genitive, as it is here, it is translated idiomatically with such terms as "worth," "great," "value," "equivalent." For example, Aeneid II, 15: "*Instar montis equus*": "a horse as great as a mountain." Thus, the translation here is "as great as all." This is to be understood in the sense that all faculties are enclosed within the forms which are supplied for them by the imagination.

16. Diem, *op. cit.,* p. 23.

17. Kierkegaard, *Sickness Unto Death,* p. 164.

18. Diem, *op. cit.,* p. 23.

19. *Ibid.,* p. 24.

20. *Ibid.* (cf. note 11).

21. In Kierkegaard's idiom, κατά takes the accusative and

means "according to." The translation here will be "according to the power."

22. Diem, *op. cit.*, p. 24.
23. *Ibid.*
24. *Ibid.*
25. *Ibid.*
26. Freud, Appendix C, *Standard Edition*, Vol. XIV, pp. 209 f.
27. *Ibid.*, pp. 213 f.
28. *Ibid.*, p. 202.

Chapter IX. *The Image:* ARTIFICER OF CONSCIOUSNESS

1. Kierkegaard, *The Journals*, No. 24, p. 20.
2. Kierkegaard, *Sickness Unto Death*, p. 164.
3. Kierkegaard, *Postscript*, p. 176.
4. *Ibid.*
5. Kierkegaard, *Sickness Unto Death*, p. 163.
6. *Ibid.*, p. 162.
7. Kierkegaard, *Concept of Dread*, p. 74.
8. Regina Olsen's brother.
9. Kierkegaard, *The Journals*, No. 396, pp. 102–103.
10. Kierkegaard, *Fear and Trembling*, p. 49.
11. Kierkegaard, *Philosophical Fragments*, p. 47.
12. Freud, *The Interpretation of Dreams*, p. 119.
13. *Ibid.*, p. 199.
14. *Ibid.*
15. *Ibid.*, p. 465.
16. *Ibid.*
17. J. Heywood Thomas, in his volume entitled *Subjectivity and Paradox* (The Macmillan Company, 1957), has provided extensive treatment of this aspect of Kierkegaard's writings. Hermann Diem (*op. cit.*, pp. 60–69) accurately recounts Kierkegaardian material on this subject. An interesting treatment that brings several points of view together and attempts to uncomplicate the Paradox is Robert E. Larsen's article "Kierkegaard's Absolute Paradox," *The Journal of Religion*, Vol. XLII (January, 1962), pp. 34–43. These treatments elab-

orate the logical and philosophical implications of the Paradox, but they overlook the psychological implications in the transforming effect that the Paradox has upon consciousness.

18. Kierkegaard, *Philosophical Fragments,* p. 15.

19. Anti-Climacus (Søren Kierkegaard), *Training in Christianity,* tr. by Walter Lowrie (Princeton University Press, 1947), pp. 124 ff.

20. *Ibid.*

21. *Ibid.,* p. 126.

22. Kierkegaard, *Philosophical Fragments,* p. 50.

23. Kierkegaard, *Training in Christianity,* p. 126.

24. Kierkegaard, *The Journals,* No. 1177, p. 425.

25. Kierkegaard, *Fear and Trembling,* pp. 49 ff.

26. It should be acknowledged at the outset that Freud and Silberer were not always of a single mind. They were in sharp disagreement over the question of what Silberer called "anagogics": the profound or morally uplifting significance of hypnagogic phenomena. However, the material presented here does not concern this point of disagreement.

27. Freud, *Interpretation of Dreams,* p. 233.

28. *Ibid.,* pp. 363–364.

29. David Rapaport, *Organization and Pathology of Thought* (Columbia University Press, 1956), p. 198.

30. Freud, *Interpretation of Dreams,* pp. 233–234.

31. Rapaport (*op. cit.,* pp. 195 ff.), has translated and annotated the core of Silberer's investigation of this type of image formation. The original is Herbert Silberer, "Über die Symbolbildung," *Jahrbuch für Psychoanalytische und Psychopathologische Forschungen,* Vol. III, 1912, pp. 661–723.

32. Silberer, "Report on a Method of Eliciting and Observing Certain Symbolic Hallucinatory-phenomena," in Rapaport, *op. cit.,* p. 198.

33. Freud, *Standard Edition,* Vol. X, p. 93n2.

34. The above explanation is taken from *Standard Edition,* Vol. X, p. 206n1. The bibliographical index to Freud's further development of this subject is given at the end of this extensive footnote.

35. Freud, *Standard Edition,* Vol. X, p. 96.

36. *Ibid.*, p. 98.

37. *Ibid.*, p. 100.

38. *Ibid.*, Vol. XII, p. 71.

39. *Ibid.*, p. 71n1.

40. *Ibid.*, Vol. XIV, p. 230.

41. *Ibid.*

42. *Ibid.*, Vol. XIII, p. 170n1; Vol. XIV, pp. 96 f.; *Interpretation of Dreams*, pp. 233, 363, 381, 414.

43. Søren Kierkegaard, *On Authority and Revelation*, tr. by Walter Lowrie (Princeton University Press, 1955), pp. 162–163.

Chapter X. RAMIFICATIONS OF THE PARADIGM: I

1. Freud, *An Outline of Psychoanalysis*, p. 122.

2. Freud, *Standard Edition*, Vol. XIV, pp. 95–97.

3. *Ibid.*, Vol. XVII, p. 194.

4. Hans Hofmann, *Religion and Mental Health* (Harper & Brothers, 1961), pp. 139 ff. This case was formerly printed in Anton T. Boisen's *Religion in Crisis and Custom* (Harper & Brothers, 1955).

5. Erik Erikson, *Childhood and Society* (W. W. Norton & Company, Inc., 1963), pp. 326 ff.

Chapter XI. RAMIFICATIONS OF THE PARADIGM: II

1. Paul Tillich, *Systematic Theology* (The University of Chicago Press, 1951), Vol. I; "The Impact of Pastoral Psychology on Theological Thought," *Pastoral Psychology*, Vol. II, No. 101 (February, 1960), pp. 17–23; "Theology and Counseling," *Journal of Pastoral Care*, Vol. X, No. 3 (Winter, 1956), pp. 193–200.

2. Erik Erikson, *Childhood and Society*, pp. 247–274. For the reader unfamiliar with Erikson, the nuclear conflict in each stage is as follows: (1) Basic Trust versus Basic Mistrust; (2) Autonomy versus Shame and Doubt; (3) Initiative versus Guilt; (4) Industry versus Inferiority; (5) Identity versus Role Confusion; (6) Intimacy versus Isolation; (7) Generativity versus Stagnation; (8) Ego Integrity versus Despair.

3. Although it is not possible at this point to develop the paradigm's application to the psychosocial and cultural milieu of the classroom, the reader will find several relevant suggestions as to the actual role that " tension " plays in learning presented in Jesse Ziegler's, *Psychology and the Teaching Church* (Abingdon Press, 1962), Ch. V.

Index